LASSETER'S REEF

ONE MAN'S JOURNEY UNCOVERS THE TRUTH

BILL DECARLI
WITH KRISTIN LEE

Published by:
Boolarong Press
38/1631 Wynnum Road
Tingalpa Qld 4173
Australia.
www.boolarongpress.com.au

First published 2021

A catalogue record for this book is available from the National Library of Australia

ISBN: 9781922643063 (paperback)

Typeset in Ibarra Real Nova 12pt by Boolarong Press

Cover, hand-painted maps and images by Belinda Williams

Cover design by Boolarong Press

Printed and bound by Watson Ferguson & Company, Tingalpa, Australia

We acknowledge and pay respect to the traditional custodians of the land, the Wangkumara people, and their elders past and present. We recognise their continuing connection to country and the area where Lasseter's Reef is situated.

Aboriginal and Torres Strait Islander readers are advised that this book may contain the names of people who have passed away.

For Mum and Dad

CONTENTS

Introduction

It is a balmy evening in late 2017. I'm standing in front of a room full of seasoned prospectors wide-eyed with wonder. For two whole hours, I have a captive audience at the Mitcham Prospectors' and Miners' Club, located in Melbourne's east. The sound of my voice is occasionally punctuated by their oohs, aahs and hearty laughter.

I've never been a member of a prospectors' or miners' club, nor received any formal training in gold and metal prospecting or detecting. Yet here I am sharing how I have solved one of Australia's greatest outback mysteries: the discovery of Lasseter's fabled gold reef.

At the end of my presentation, everyone stands up, clapping and cheering. Then, one after the other, they come up to me smiling eagerly as they firmly shake my hand and offer their sincere congratulations. Not one person in that room questions my discovery. They believe that I have found Lasseter's Reef.

Ever since gold-seeker Harold Bell Lasseter publicly claimed that he'd found his fabulous seam of gold in Central Australia somewhere near the turn of the twentieth century, it has become one of Australia's most persistent and controversial tales. For me, though, it feels good to be able to finally share the entire truth. But getting to this point has been an extraordinarily lengthy journey.

I was just a few months shy of my twentieth birthday when I first heard about the legendary gold deposit. I was living in a caravan with ribbed aluminum cladding in the backyard of my future in-laws at Research, on Melbourne's rural-urban fringe, and they were encouraging me to go and work in the mines in Western Australia.

There was a resources boom there in the 1960s. In addition to iron ore, there were discoveries of nickel, oil, gas, bauxite and alumina. The gold mining, at that stage, had gone into decline. My future mother-in-law half-jokingly suggested, 'Why don't you go and search for Lasseter's Reef while you're there.' In between jobs at the time, I thought, why not go to Western Australia? It could be an adventure.

It took me three-and-a-half days to drive with my then-Border Collie from Melbourne to Perth. I drove via the flat, almost treeless Nullarbor Plain. A seemingly boundless limestone plateau that is continuously smoothed by wind and rain, it stretches between the little fishing town of Ceduna on the Eyre Peninsula in South Australia and the even tinier gold mining town of Norseman in Western Australia.

It was just before the first section of the 1660-kilometre long and lonely Eyre Highway was to be sealed, and my mud-splattered Holden HR sedan was the first vehicle to be let through in three weeks. The highway had been flooded and various vehicles, including monstrous road trains, were still stuck in deep mud holes. Under dark, glowering skies, I continued driving west.

By the time I arrived in Perth, the rain was hammering down. I put the car in for a service, then went to have something to eat. After returning to the mechanic to pick up my car, I started the engine and, with the windscreen wipers going full pelt, drove straight back to Melbourne. At first, I put it down to the gloomy weather and me being homesick, young and foolish. The truth was, I felt like I didn't belong there. Instead, I joined the army.

As for Lasseter's Reef, it was to be another thirteen years before I thought about it again. What initially seemed to be a meaningful reminder, or perhaps even a meaningful distraction, suddenly became all-consuming: I wanted to sate my curiosity and prove that the reef wasn't a myth; it existed. Moreover, it wasn't where anyone thought it was.

Whether it was simple logic or intuition — although some might say I'd completely lost my mind — that led me into the endless expanse of outback wilderness, by August 1991 I was standing on a 16-kilometre long reef with large quartz outcrops that was surrounded by sandy red earth plains dotted liberally with mulga trees. Filled with astonishment and exhilaration, in the distance I could see the three tall circular hills that, according to Lasseter, 'could not be mistaken'.[1]

Between triple-checking my map and keenly scanning the vast, remote, fiery red desert landscape, everything was just as he'd indicated, based on an interpretation of key documentation and his rather fragmented diary that contains sketches and written accounts of his final, lonely journey. Yet where I was standing was a long way from where he or anyone else had ever searched for it.

How did I find it?

Of the few hundred explorers that have attempted to find the lost gold reef since Lasseter's ill-fated 1930–1931 expedition, I went on a hunch: to find the pivotal landmarks Lasseter had clearly described; however, in the opposite direction.

Although it was always about proving my theory that the reef existed, not so much about finding the gold, I've returned to the site another nine times. I've also discovered, by happenstance, a curious link between Lasseter and a mysterious bushman, further reinforcing the reef's location.

Why hasn't any of this been revealed before?

Despite having found the reef and generating some interest, until recently my forty-year journey with Lasseter's Reef has been somewhat erratic, at times even disappointing. Some are intrigued about the myth and legend of Lasseter's Reef; others simply don't believe that it exists. Then there are those who think this is one Australian mystery that doesn't need to be solved. Folklore, after all, is what stirs and shapes our psyche.

Throughout all of this, a syndicate was formed with the intention of excavating the gold but then disbanded. Shortly afterwards, an exploration licence was taken out for the reef with a mining company; however, the main area of interest was declared Aboriginal sacred land. Then our family business went up in flames and we lost our home. I wondered if Lasseter's Reef was meant to be found after all.

Even when I completely let go of all hope of being able to do anything more, for whatever reason, I never stopped talking about it. Sometimes it was as if someone was behind me, prodding and urging me to keep going. In 2005, and with the assistance of writer Angie Testa, I co-authored my first book, *A Dead Man's Dream: Lasseter's Reef Found.* Although I could have revised it, based on significant new information and mind-blowing insights, I decided to start this book about my journey with Lasseter's Reef from scratch.

For too long, Lasseter's Reef has been over-romanticised. So many people were, and still are, simply lured by the gold. Just like Chinese whispers, the stories surrounding it have become so warped that we lost sight of the truth. For me, it was time to right all the wrongs of those tales told over the last century. The more I delved into Lasseter's story, the more my own version of events got stronger. Every single piece of new evidence fortifies the reef's existence. But ultimately it was the land that held the answers.

Besides, as someone who values honour and honesty, I believe it is important to be fair and remember people's contributions. Most importantly, we remember people for who they are. Sure, Lasseter has already been commemorated in a number of ways, especially in the Northern Territory. There is a highway, a hotel casino, the cave where he took shelter, a memorial cairn at Irving Creek where he died, and the rugged country where he believed the reef was have all been named in his honour. Fittingly, the inscription on the front plaque of Lasseter's final resting place at Alice Springs, which I visited with my wife Pat during our 30th wedding anniversary, echoes some of the words from Theodore Roosevelt's stirring 1910 speech, "The Man in the Arena":

> It is not the critic who counts, or how the strong man stumbled and fell
> Or where the doer of deeds could have done better.
> The credit belongs to the man who is actually in the arena
> Who knows the great enthusiasms, the great devotion
> And spends himself in a worthy cause.
> If he fails, at least he fails by daring greatly,
> So that he will never be one of those cold and timid souls
> Who know neither victory or defeat.[2]

There is no doubt that Lasseter had a pioneering spirit, but everything that led him to that Central Australian gold expedition to the west of Alice Springs was, as I reveal, all due to a combination of circumstance, misunderstandings and a mistake. Although some regard Lasseter as a rogue and an illywhacker, from the outset I didn't want to judge or label him based on other people's hearsay. I wanted to find out why a man would go out into Australia's harsh dry interior in search of a mother lode, which ultimately cost him his life. No one goes into a forbidding and hostile desert without good reason.

Like someone attempting to solve a cold case, I wanted to know as much as possible about Lasseter and his connection to a man whose name had been mentioned throughout history, yet somehow got disregarded. It was there that I found the startling answers and felt compelled to rightfully acknowledge the true roles that both of these men played with the reef's existence.

In the process, it has also been a personally healing journey, a resetting of my inner compass, inadvertently helping me breakthrough post-traumatic stress disorder. I was a troubled man when I came back from the Vietnam War, but I didn't know why my psychological and emotional equilibrium had become so imbalanced. Through getting to know Lasseter, and deepening my connection to the land, I started to understand myself.

Since 2017, my interest in sharing the real story about Lasseter's Reef has been renewed. With so many books, documentaries and theories, even songs, plays and poetry circulating since Lasseter's death in 1931, it would be reasonable for you to think here's another idiot who reckons he's found Lasseter's Reef. Therefore, I ask you, dear reader, to keep an open mind as you peruse my account of events so that you may draw your own conclusions.

Not only is it time to put the myth of Lasseter's Reef to rest once and for all, it is the beginning of a new chapter that more Australians, including local communities surrounding the reef, can benefit from.

CHAPTER 1

THE CURIOUS CASE OF LASSETER

The night was cold. My right ankle was swollen and throbbing. It was 1980 and I was lying on the couch in the lounge room with my feet propped up on a couple of firm pillows, half-watching TV. I was in the midst of a painful and mind-numbing recovery from an intensely challenging surgery on my ankle that had only taken place a few days beforehand.

Slowly, my heavy eyelids opened and shut. Despite the sharp, stabbing pain, for a rare moment I was on the precipice of sinking into a profoundly deep sleep. Then suddenly, I heard journalist Mike Willesee's trademark voice: calm with measured pauses. He was talking, on TV, about Australian legends and historical figures, from notorious bushranger Ned Kelly to hapless explorers Burke and Wills.

When I heard Willesee say 'Lasseter's Reef', my eyes jolted wide open.

Although I'd first heard of the legendary gold reef from my former in-laws thirteen years prior, until then it had been pushed into the dim recesses of my mind, where it had been long-forgotten. But as Willesee continued presenting the in-depth documentary called *The Legend of Lasseter,* I couldn't peel my eyes away from the screen. He was retracing the steps of the disastrous Central Australian Gold Exploration (CAGE) Company expedition to Central Australia from 1930 to 1931. Mostly, he was investigating the circumstances surrounding Harold Bell Lasseter's death and sorting fact from fiction with regards to the reef.

I've always enjoyed the sense of adventure, storytelling and contradictions that have occurred throughout Australian history, but I quickly realised that there was more to what at first seems a remarkably far-fetched story: one that is inevitably larger than the reef itself.

For starters, Lasseter claimed that in 1897, as a seventeen-year-old boy, he travelled solo on horseback from Cairns via Cloncurry in Queensland to the MacDonnell Ranges in Central Australia. His reason for wandering in the searing desert heat of the isolated outback was to prospect for rich blood-red rubies. As it turned out, they were worthless garnets.

After stopping at the frontier town of Alice Springs for much-needed supplies, Lasseter continued his journey west through the MacDonnell Ranges with his two horses. It was while he was heading towards the coast of Western Australia, either to Fremantle or Carnarvon to work on coastal steamers, that he miscalculated the distance and directions. Some maps, as Lasseter subsequently stated, were known to be half-done and unreliable back then:

> According to the maps of those days the MacDonnells extended to the sea, so I thought I did not have much farther to go. More weeks passed, and still I did not reach the sea. I was now in the heart of the desert, and the country seemed to be getting worse. I had come to the end of the MacDonnells and ahead of me lay miles of red sandhills covered with thorny spinifex. I veered slightly south-west and struck more mountains but no coastline. Food was getting low, and my position was becoming desperate. Then I ran into more sandhill country and the water gave out. I struggled on and again ran into mountainous country, eventually coming across a waterhole. I made camp here and had a good spell. Finally, I decided to push on. The sea could not be far off now.[1]

To his astonishment, though, he stumbled on a sizeable gold-studded reef.

Now according to Lasseter, it had a large quartz outcrop and a heap of stones, which had the most peculiar colour: a milky green coloured quartz with ironstone inclusion. Cracking them open, they were filled with long, shiny gold veins.

Then, as he scanned the area, he realised the reef they had come from was a staggering 10 miles long. By my calculations, that's about ten times longer than the length of Melbourne's CBD!

On top of that, the reef was 4 to 7 feet high and up to 12 feet wide. Excited, Lasseter gathered samples in an oatmeal bag and duly noted the reef's location near the border. However, his fortuitous find was short-lived — his supplies depleted rapidly and his horses perished from thirst and exhaustion.

With no water and little food, a starving, dishevelled Lasseter staggered through the dry, hard-baked desert and under a merciless, hot sun. Hopelessly lost and on the brink of death, he was found by an Afghan cameleer. He then took an ailing Lasseter, who was still clutching his bag of gold specimens, on a camel to the camp of a government surveyor with the surname of Harding.

Attributing Harding as the man who cared for him and took him to Carnarvon, Lasseter shared the details of his fabulously rich find. Completely agog, Harding declared that the samples were the finest he'd ever seen; he was keen for Lasseter to take him out to the reef as soon as possible. But the young treasure hunter was in no hurry to go back out there. 'Haunted by the nightmare of my dreadful experience, I refused,' Lasseter recalled several years later.[2]

Besides needing to recover from his traumatic desert experience, Lasseter wanted to spend a few years in the Western Australian goldfields to gain hands-on experience. During this time, Lasseter and Harding stayed in contact. Then, in 1900, the two men departed with camels from Carnarvon and headed straight to Central Australia, where they, miraculously, relocated the reef.

Although they took samples and bearings at the site, when both of them returned to Carnarvon, which is about

700 miles west of where Lasseter indicated that the gold reef lay, they realised that their watches were about an hour and a quarter out. Not surprisingly, it rendered the readings from the sextant (a navigation instrument) that Harding used as inaccurate. Despite this, it is said that Harding registered the gold samples — which assayed 3 ounces to the ton — in his name in Perth.

With neither Lasseter nor Harding able to source any funding to survey the reef, particularly with Western Australia's gold rush being in focus at the time, Harding is thought to have ventured to Adelaide, then Melbourne and finally London to seek financial support. It never eventuated, though. It is said that he died, either while he was abroad or shortly after he returned to Australia.

For some time, Lasseter kept his lucrative find to himself. Instead, he headed to America, where he met and subsequently married Florence Elizabeth Scott in New York in December 1903. Four years later, he became an American citizen. While living there, it is believed that he converted to Mormonism, although I eventually discovered that there was no official record of him actually doing so. It seems that his real faith was the Church of England.[3]

In late 1909, Lasseter, Florence and their first daughter, Lillian (nicknamed Ruby), came to Australia. After a short stop in Adelaide, they moved to Tabulam in northern New South Wales, where their second daughter, Beulah, was born. Moving around became a habit for Lasseter. He also did various jobs. While he had a wandering spirit, I could tell that he was an unsettled man.

In 1916, this short and stockily built dilettante enlisted in the army in Melbourne, but that was fleeting, and somewhat convoluted. The following year, he reenlisted in the army in Adelaide. However, he suffered a head injury — due to 'unwittingly' getting involved in a brawl — which may have caused some memory loss and possible delusions. It was hardly surprising that shortly afterwards he was deemed medically unfit.

In January 1924, he had another marriage to Louise Irene (Rene) Lillywhite in Melbourne. He and Rene had three children, namely Robert, Betty and Joy. I was astounded, though, when I found out that Lasseter worked on two major Australian building projects: the first one being at the new Parliament House site in Canberra, where he worked as a carpenter. He then worked on the Sydney Harbour Bridge during its construction. However, he was dismissed for disputing how he believed it should be built.

Afterwards, he managed a pottery workshop, located in Redfern, for limbless soldiers. His interests and talents were mind-boggling.

Add to that how Lasseter was a prolific and creative writer. He frequently had letters or his opinions about various community matters or personal ideas published in newspapers

Born Lewis Hubert Lasseter, in 1924 he changed his name to Harold Bell Lasseter. (Author's collection)

and periodicals. Alternatively, he was writing to various government departments, with the intention to garner support for one of his grandiose schemes.

What I thought was particularly interesting was that it wasn't until 14 October 1929 (two days after the Australian Labor Party returned to office, and the week before the Wall Street Crash which triggered the Great Depression) that Lasseter decided to create public interest in his discovery of the enormous gold-bearing reef. In order to secure the gold, he believed that £5 million was required (the equivalent to almost a billion dollars today), along with a sufficient supply of water to tap into it.

Lasseter wrote to Albert E. "Texas" Green, the Labor member for Kalgoorlie in Western Australia, firstly to offer his 'fraternal congratulations', but mostly to outline his extraordinary find in the brutal desert. He also offered to survey a route for a pipeline — for a fee of £2000.[4] Somewhat intrigued, Green, who was promptly appointed as Minister of Defence and was no longer in a position to do anything about Lasseter's proposal, forwarded the letter to the chairman of the Development and Migration Commission, Herbert Gepp, to see what he thought. If anyone knew how to handle a matter like this, it was him.

After Gepp and a colleague, Dr Leonard Keith Ward, a government geologist, eventually nailed down an interview with Lasseter in Sydney, they submitted what became known as the Gepp Report.

Still waiting for a response, a restlessly eager Lasseter wrote another letter to Gepp in January 1930. In it, he declared:

> I have reason to believe that the area in which the reef is situated is covered by the Aborigines reserve, so I took a trip to Canberra to enquire of the Home & Territories Dept if we would be allowed to work the reef should it prove to be therein. I received a sympathetic hearing but believe it is a matter which you would be in a better position to handle than

myself; so I thought I would drop you a line with that end in view.[5]

Despite his persistent letter writing, and curious officials not being able to do a thorough search of what was deemed a vaguely proposed and highly unlikely area, the Western Australian government declined to fund his survey expedition. Lasseter had to rethink his approach. However, with what eventuated next, had he been redirected?

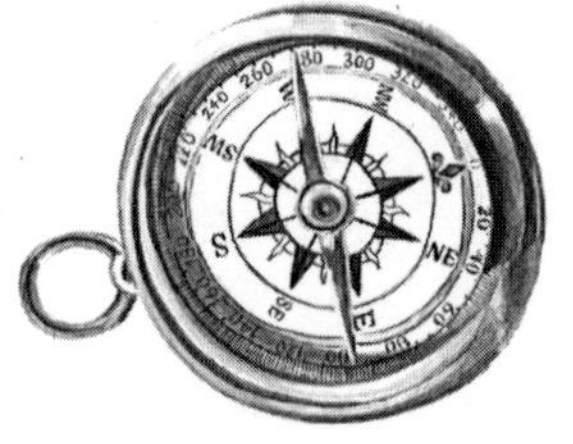

Chapter 2
A Beacon of Hope

The impact of the Great Depression was harsh and soul destroying. Hunger, exhaustion and despair filled the eyes of shabbily dressed men, women and children. Each day, men would walk aimlessly for miles. From large, overcrowded cities to pint-sized country towns, they were desperately hoping to find work, even if it was odd jobs on farms to provide a skerrick of food for themselves and their families. So many people were homeless and often resorted to constructing tiny makeshift shelters made from a combination of scrap metal and large, empty hessian sacks.

But a determined Harold Bell Lasseter, who was on the brink of losing his home, had another idea, an ingenious idea, to help get himself and the nation out of their economic doldrums. It was sometime in April 1930 when he approached the Australian Workers Union (AWU) office in Pitt Street, Sydney. Lasseter went to see its president, John "Jack" Bailey, a former New South Wales politician who had been expelled from the Labor Party.

On the day Lasseter appeared 'unannounced' at the AWU office, Bailey and his son, Ernest, along with journalist Errol Coote and the union's state mining secretary, Jack Jenkins, were in attendance. Lasseter confidently pitched the 'rich reef of gold' as being the world's largest gold producer. That was a mighty big call. In view of initially receiving some guffaws, Lasseter retorted half defiantly, 'You may laugh ... but I'm not here on a cock and bull story. I have the real thing. I found it there myself.'[1] As he continued his story, the four other men's eyes glistened like shiny gold.

At a time of significant hardship, the gold reef, which Jenkins estimated to have a staggering value of £66 million, was *seen* as a possible economic saviour. No wonder it called for further investigation.

Despite Lasseter not revealing the reef's *exact* location, largely due to the incorrect readings he and Harding had taken thirty years prior, several intensive cross-examinations found sufficient findings to support his remarkable claim. Lasseter convinced the gold-stricken board that he could relocate the reef by relying on his memory of the landmarks. It must have been one hell of a conversation.

To confirm the reef's existence, John Bailey made enquiries with the Department of Mines in Canberra. He discovered that there was indeed a reef in the region Lasseter had described:

> I searched the records for Lasseter's Reef. There were no records of any reef being held by Lasseter. The records did disclose that in the vicinity mentioned by Lasseter there was a reef known as Harding's Reef and that two expeditions had proceeded from [the] West Australian side to locate it, but both expeditions had struck hostile natives, and some of the members of the expedition were speared by the natives and camels also. Some of the men and camels died, and those who had escaped had great difficulty getting back.[2]

Next a syndicate needed to be formed to raise the all-important capital. John Bailey invited fifty associates along to a meeting, to discuss Lasseter's scheme and the formation of a company. All bar one were convinced that Lasseter had stumbled across something so extraordinary. Aviator Charles Ulm, who completed the first trans-Pacific flight to Australia with Sir Charles Kingsford Smith, was in attendance. He was dubious about the reef's location. Based on Lasseter explaining that his and Harding's readings were inaccurate when they ventured across the desert from Carnarvon, Ulm concluded, 'That in turn means that on your bearings the reef must be somewhere in the Indian Ocean.'

Without hesitation, Lasseter explained that the bearings were useless, it was the landmarks etched in his memory that would reveal the location. Still unconvinced, Ulm then added, '... I am afraid those landmarks would have become slightly hazy in the mental picture, after all this time.'[3] Yet Ulm's probing curiosity didn't dampen the room's jubilant mood whatsoever. There was gold to be found, and tons of it.

CAGE was then, according to Ernest Bailey, formed in about all of 'ten minutes'.[4] Ernest took on the role of company secretary, while his father, John Bailey, became its chairman.

At the same time that CAGE was announced publically in May, a gleeful Lasseter wrote to Herbert Gepp, wondering if he was interested in becoming a syndicate member:

> Dear Sir, I presume you have seen the newspaper splash re Eldorado in Central Australia. This was really a surprise to me as I was asking Bailey's assistance to get the Minister's consent to prospect the [Aboriginal] reserve in Central Australia and he took the initiative re forming a syndicate. Anyway he spilt the beans as far as keeping it quiet is concerned, so now it is up to me to get there as soon as possible. Still I do not think the plane is the best way, and maybe I can get them to adopt my idea of using a six-wheeled truck. If you care to have a finger in the pie the Syndicate consists of 50 shares at £50 each paid to £20 with calls of £5 as required.[5]

Although it is highly unlikely that Gepp made any financial contributions, very swiftly £5000 was raised, which, as I found out later, was allegedly acquired through AWU members' funds. It seems that nothing was going to stand in the way of the large-scale CAGE expedition, which officially commenced from Alice Springs on 24 July 1930, despite some accounts stating that it was a few days earlier.

The original six-man expedition party was led by prospector Fred Blakeley, also dubbed the 'Bicycle Bushman', having cycled about 2200 miles (3540 kilometres) from White Cliffs, New South Wales, to Darwin with the O'Neil brothers in 1908. Blakeley was the brother of the Minister for Home Affairs and former AWU president Arthur Blakeley, who'd already seen the Gepp Report before CAGE was established.

Other expedition members included surveyor George Sutherland; driver and mechanic Phil Taylor; governor general's aide Captain Blakiston-Houston; Coote as deputy leader and the pilot, despite being trained but not having a current licence; and Lasseter, nicknamed Harry and Possum, as a paid guide. Then Alice Springs prospector Fred Colson was added to the unwonted mix, by Blakeley, to provide a backup truck, while Mickey the half-blind Aboriginal guide was engaged from a dried-up cattle station shortly after the expedition had set off.

Among their provisions and equipment were two trucks, including a two-and-a-half ton Thornycroft truck that had been donated for the expedition and Colson's Chev truck. There was also a wireless radio transmitter and a plane aptly renamed the *Golden Quest*, for Coote to take Lasseter on reconnaissance flights. It was deemed to be the best-equipped expedition to the 'dead heart' of Australia at the time.

However, it was also when central and southern Australia were in the grip of a savage drought. Not exactly conducive for an intrepid exploration heading north-west from Alice Springs. Nonetheless, after spending almost five days heaving, loading and shoving the heavy equipment on the trucks, it wasn't long after they departed the Alice that the vehicles repeatedly ploughed into deep sand dunes. The only way out was to constantly dig the bogged vehicles out by shovel and hand. And when they weren't laying down coconut matting to inch their way through the saltbush or across dry creek beds, they were repairing tyre punctures or replacing shredded tyres due to the razor-sharp spikes in thick mulga. It was nothing short of hellish.

In addition, they had mechanical breakdowns or ran out of fuel. At one stage, the mighty, six-wheeled Thornycroft caught fire. That truck was no match for the Australian desert. Having sufficient water, particularly in the drought-stricken outback, was a constant issue. It was excruciatingly slow going with the men taking nine days to travel 240 miles from Alice Springs to Taylor's Creek. The creek was unofficially named by Blakeley at the time but is correctly known as Aiai Creek, or sometimes written as Yaiyai or even Yaya Creek.

A makeshift airstrip was then constructed there and Blakiston-Houston left to return to civilisation, as originally intended, on the plane. Coote then flew back to rejoin the expedition a few days later. However, the size of the airstrip was too small for landing. As a result, the *Golden Quest* skimmed a tree and nearly crash landed into the creek.

With urgent repairs needed, the men had to wait before they could continue the expedition to Ilbilla, their proposed base camp. After the plane was fixed, it was tied down (to be retrieved later) and the expedition resumed. However, the tension mounted between Lasseter and Blakeley, especially as to which direction to take along the imposing Haasts Bluff monolith: north or south?

Lasseter recalled travelling along the southern side when he first claimed to be there in 1897. Meanwhile, Blakeley insisted that they stick with the original plan of going along the northern side, which was where they ended up travelling. Despite their snail-like progress, eventually the weary men arrived and set up camp at Ilbilla. From then on, the friction remained high and morale plummeted, with Lasseter often choosing to keep to himself.

About a week later, Coote and Colson returned to Aiai Creek to bring back the *Golden Quest*. As it was taking off, it stalled and careened into a gum tree, ripping off a wing and injuring Coote. With a nasty gash to his leg, cracked ribs and various other injuries, he then had to be driven by Colson in his truck to Alice Springs for urgent medical attention. Originally the plan was that if Coote didn't return to Ilbilla by the end of three full days, the expedition members would send out a search party.

Given there was no sign of him with the plane, Blakeley, Sutherland and Taylor returned to Aiai Creek, while Lasseter and Mickey the Aboriginal guide remained at the camp. After five punishing days, the three men arrived at Aiai Creek to find the battered aircraft and a note advising of the accident. A few days later, they returned to Ilbilla, with the broken plane in tow.

While Coote was recovering in hospital, a DH 60 Moth biplane, which became known as *Golden Quest II*, was organised by the CAGE directors in Sydney, and much to the chagrin of Blakeley. The replacement aircraft was flown directly to Alice Springs by a new pilot, Pat Hall.

While Coote and Hall were preparing to fly out to meet with the others, the expedition edged its way towards the Western Australian border. Meanwhile, the tension between Lasseter and Blakeley became increasingly inflammatory. When the pair made the taxing, perilous climb to the top of Mount Marjorie (now known as Mount Leisler) to take a bearing with the sextant, Lasseter felt they were off course. By his calculations, they needed to be in the Petermann Ranges, not so far north. That meant heading 150 miles south.

Since Blakeley was familiar with the mysterious looking ranges, he didn't believe it was possible for a gold reef, like Lasseter had described, to exist there. He didn't think Lasseter knew where he was going. He started to question if he'd visited the area at all. Not even camels dared to tread in that wild rugged country. Frustrated, Lasseter indicated that it would be much easier to find the reef if they'd approached it from the west, as he had done all those years ago when he relocated it with Harding.

That night, after yet another fruitless attempt to relocate the reef, Blakeley recalled:

> I had a bit of a feed and then turned in, for I was greatly troubled. The show today had been that of a simple child. I could not pin Harry down to anything definite. I lay there and thought. I worked it out that a man who was supposed to have been here twice should be able to recognise the lay of the country from such elevated positions as we had been in. I felt certain by all his actions that this was Harry's first visit to this country.[6]

While the expedition was punishing and its members were a peculiar bunch, I thought it was interesting when Phil Taylor, the only surviving CAGE expedition member who was interviewed in *The Legend of Lasseter* documentary, also said that he had serious doubts about Lasseter. Besides wondering if he'd 'ever been in that country at all before', Taylor described Lasseter as a 'funny sort of chap' who could be quite genial one minute, then 'pick a fight over absolutely nothing'.[7]

Given the rather dodgy setup, I thought Lasseter had every right to be suspicious of the others.

With the terrain becoming almost impassable, the expedition party was forced to return to Ilbilla. When they arrived there, they were surprised to see a young man by the name of Paul Johns, a German dingo scalper, with two Aboriginal guides and a string of camels. Johns, who'd apparently heard about the expedition, offered his services to help the men. These ships of the desert were, after all, a far more appropriate mode of transport for their purpose. However, Johns was declined.

Despite his presence creating unease among the expedition party, Blakeley encouraged Johns and his Aboriginal companions to linger around the camp for a few weeks. He thought they could be a potential backup while the expedition continued to find those all-important landmarks. If Johns and his team were needed, Blakeley would send up signal flares.

By that stage, pilots Coote and Hall had rejoined the expedition with the *Golden Quest II*. Hall took Lasseter on a reconnaissance flight to see if the reef could be viewed from the air. But when the pair returned to camp and were bombarded with questions, Lasseter, while shaking his head, told the other expedition members that he didn't see the reef. He still believed that they were too far north.

Coote didn't buy it. Later on, he pulled Lasseter aside to remind him of his obligation to share the reef's location with the company shareholders. Despite explaining his reasons for not doing so, largely because he didn't trust Blakeley, Lasseter confided to Coote that he *had* seen the reef.

Squatting down, Lasseter drew a map in the desert sand with a stick. It included Lake Christopher in Western Australia as a radial point, and some other key landmarks, most notably the three distinctive hills, which he called the 'Three Sisters'. Not quite sure what to make of this illuminating information, Coote said that Lasseter was still required to tell the other CAGE members. But a wary Lasseter indicated that he would divulge the details all in good time. He even made a point of telling Coote that it was impossible to land a plane anywhere near the reef.

Yet when Coote pressed Hall for more details about the reconnaissance flight, Hall suddenly remembered:

> We must have been gone about an hour and ten minutes when he [Lasseter] started to jump about in the front cockpit very excitedly. He pointed at something but I did not know what he was trying to tell me. He almost hopped out of the plane. There was no doubt that he was genuinely excited. Then he waved to me to return.[8]

Stunned, Coote wondered suspiciously if Lasseter was right after all, but remained mum, for the time being, anyway.

With the expedition continuing to the south, the country became increasingly treacherous and forbidding. As usual, Blakeley was completely miffed by Lasseter's lack of knowing where he was going, let alone his refusal to share any information about the reef's location. He decided that it was time to abandon the expedition. All of the CAGE expedition members needed to return to Alice Springs — pronto. However, Lasseter vehemently insisted that he continue with Johns, his two guides and five trusty camels to find the reef.

With Blakeley reluctantly agreeing to sign Johns on for two months, if they didn't return by the first half of November, he would send out a search party. But was Blakeley giving Lasseter an out? Prior to their departure, though, and without Blakeley knowing, Johns' two guides had disappeared. Something else Blakeley wasn't aware of at the time was that Lasseter had already sent a telegram to the CAGE directors in Sydney, indicating that he'd found the reef!

CHAPTER 3
TRAGEDY STRIKES

On the morning of September 15, Lasseter and Paul Johns quietly left camp with the team of five slow-plodding and heavily loaded camels. Initially they headed in a south-westerly direction but there was no water to be found in the immensely difficult sandhill country. Their only option was to take a tiring and time-consuming detour to the north-east.

Ten days later, they arrived at the thick salt-encrusted Lake Amadeus. With its surface coated in brilliant, blinding white, it appeared safe enough to cross. The pair figured that they could use it as a shortcut to get to Mount Olga. They weren't even halfway across when the lake's surface cracked, with the camels slipping knee-deep into the treacherous bog.

As Johns vividly recalled of that near fatal decision in an interview with journalist Ernestine Hill a couple of years afterwards (although not actually published until 1968), 'The heavily laden camels, paralysed with fright, were slowly sinking into the quagmire. Frantically unslinging their loadings, straining at the trappings and nose lines, shouting and cursing, we finally succeeded in freeing the animals from the mire.'[1]

Two days later, the exhausted men and sore-footed camels arrived at Mount Olga, where they rested by a waterhole. Lasseter then left Johns for a couple of days to scout ahead on foot. When he returned, he told Johns that he'd found the reef, but didn't reveal its location. Nor did he show him any of the samples that he'd taken.

Like the others, Johns was suspicious of Lasseter's so-called knowledge of the area. In this case, though, he called Lasseter a liar. Unimpressed, the nuggetty little man hurled a plate filled with tinned fruit directly at Johns' face. A heated row ensued, with Johns drawing his revolver. Somehow, Lasseter managed to wrench it from him, although injuring his hand in the process. The hammer had gotten jammed between his thumb and finger. He then tossed the gun into the thorny bushes.

Despite the stand-off, the pair came to an arrangement. By this stage, they needed to return to the food dump at Ilbilla. They were running desperately low on supplies. When they arrived there, Lasseter requested that Johns return to Alice Springs to send some letters that he'd already written. One of them was for the CAGE directors, again indicating that he'd recovered his lost reef, but this time he'd pegged it. He also explained in the letter that the reef wasn't as rich as he'd anticipated, and that he would only be a few weeks away at most. He and Johns were due to reconnect within four to six weeks.

With two camels and fresh supplies, Lasseter headed for Lake Christopher, located to the west of the Rawlinson Ranges in Western Australia, which are about 100 miles from the border. Evidently he arrived there, given he marked 'Lasseter — 2/12/30' on a tree. It was found a couple of years later by English-born author and explorer Michael Terry, who'd spoken with some local Aboriginal people indicating that a white man had previously camped there. Perhaps Terry was on a similar quest to the CAGE expedition.

While Lasseter waited out in the desert, Blakeley had been fired for abandoning Lasseter, and Coote was instated as expedition leader. He was, supposedly, searching for Lasseter. However, Coote didn't fully outline his plans to the CAGE directors about building an airstrip at Ayers Rock (Uluru), where he ended up being stranded with the plane for some weeks after its propeller got damaged.

I was dumbfounded when I found out that a large-scale search, including the use of the Royal Australian Air Force, was underway for Coote, but why wasn't it for Lasseter? Coote was found, eventually, and his services terminated.

As for Lasseter, in the event something went wrong during the expedition, a Swedish man by the name of Olof Johanson was to be sent to meet with him at Lake Christopher. Johanson happened to be working in Boulder, a town in the Western Australian goldfields bordering Kalgoorlie (now known as Kalgoorlie-Boulder), while Lasseter was on the expedition.

In what was to become known as his diary, and as I explain in due course, Lasseter believed that Johanson had stumbled on the exact same reef. It was later on when a note was found at a burnt-out campsite at Ayers Rock, which had been signed by Johanson and another man called Smith, that indicated Lasseter needed assistance. As it turned out, the rendezvous never happened.

On about December 27, while Lasseter was thought to be somewhere in the sandhills near the Hull River, his camels spooked and bolted. They took his precious food and water with them.

Like a race starter's gun being fired inside my head, my mind galloped at the thought of this tragic mishap when I first heard about it. Then suddenly, I slapped my hand down on the couch and yelled out, 'Lasseter was in the wrong place. The reef isn't there! It's on the other side.'

While the entire CAGE expedition was fraught with accidents, desperation and deception, I knew that the reef's location had to be a reversal of bearing, or what is more commonly known as a reference reversal. A well-used army technique, its purpose is to hide the exact location of something significant, be it troops, civilians or key landmarks. It was also used by prospectors to protect their rich finds. That way, if the enemy or anyone else picks up on the location, they would be travelling the same distance but in the opposite direction. They would never find whatever they'd set out to seek, which, as I explain in later chapters, is exactly what happened with Lasseter.

At this stage, I believed that Lasseter had found the reef all those years ago, he'd just forgotten where the landmarks were, especially since he'd previously suffered a head injury. Why else would a man go on a gruelling desert expedition, let alone convince the AWU to back him?

As for my reference reversal theory, I excitedly shouted to my wife Pat, 'Hon, can you bring me the atlas of Australia?'

Poking her head into the room, wondering what all the commotion was, she looked at me with a furrowed brow and asked, 'Did you say you wanted an atlas?'

'I sure do!' I hastily replied.

'What on earth for?'

When Pat returned with the atlas, I flipped it open it to the map of Central Australia, then circled a section of it with a red pen, according to the distance Lasseter had indicated: 300 miles from Alice Springs. In my case, though, I circled it to the south-east. I didn't want to focus on the south-west like Lasseter had previously done. I figured this eastern direction, which was closer to the Queensland border, was where the reef was.

As for Lasseter, he was left to die in the desert. Found wandering by some members of the Pitjantjatjara tribe, he was thought to be suffering from dysentery and was partially blinded by sandy blight. Despite some confrontation and being threatened with spears, other tribe members, including an elder with distinctive warts, "Old Warts", guided him to a nearby cave (later known as Lasseter's Cave) on the banks of the Hull River to recuperate.

There, Lasseter remained ever hopeful that his rescue party would arrive soon. They never came.

While spending what is believed to have been most of January 1931 at the cave, Lasseter purportedly recorded haphazard notes to his wife, Rene. These notes ultimately became known as Lasseter's Diary, which I read extracts of not long after watching the documentary. In some parts, it reads like a tragic adventure, but overall the words are a harrowing read, particularly when he wrote about his miserable demise:

> How I long to see my children once more, to hold their chubby hands and to see their laughing faces and hear their baby prattle. My God why does not help come, with lots of water I can hold out for several days yet but the agony of starvation may drive me to shoot myself. I think it the worst possible death ... I should never have gone on alone ... What good a reef worth millions? I would give it all for a loaf of bread.[2]

But what I found most startling among his scrawlings, especially in view of my reversal of bearing theory, was when he revealed that he'd pegged the reef:

> Darling I've pegged the reef and marked the exact locality on the map which is buried in my kit ... on the sandhills where the camels bolted — on the east side of the hill, and I photographed the datum peg dated 23rd December. I can't understand ... support or relief has not been afforded me ... I buried 3 rolls of film in a 5 lb treacle tin on the sandhills too.[3]

And yet again he mentioned it, although this time indicated that the peg *may not* be there:

> Rene darling. Don't grieve for me I've done my best & have pegged the reef, not strictly according to law because the blacks pinched my miners right & I don't know the number but I photographed the datum post on the Quartz Blow. The post is sticking in a water hole & the photo faces north. I made the run in 5 days but the blacks have a sacred place nearby & will pull the peg up for sure. I have taken the films

> and planted them at Wintersglen if I can get there the blight has got me beat ...[4]

Despite Lasseter wasting away, later in the month, and with the assistance of some friendly Aboriginals, he set off for Mount Olga. His reason for going there was to meet the relief party. However, it was 81 miles away and he scarcely had any water. It is said that he got as far as Irving Creek in the Petermann Ranges, where he perished on what was believed to be about January 30.

Apparently a search party for Lasseter was sent out by CAGE from Alice Springs to Ilbilla on 27 November 1930. It included Phil Taylor as the expedition's newly appointed leader. He was accompanied by Paul Johns, given he was the last known white man to see Lasseter alive.

Before departing, Taylor and Johns had to wait for the arrival of the *Golden Quest II*, which had a new pilot and engineer. But that too was filled with a series of incidents and mishaps, with the plane going missing. It required its own search party.

In the first half of February 1931, Taylor and Johns continued the search for Lasseter with camels. However, Taylor fell ill. They were then forced to return to Hermannsburg Mission, about 78 miles south-west of Alice Springs.

Afterwards, CAGE sent experienced pastoralist and bushman Bob Buck to find Lasseter, although his departure was delayed — he was waiting for a crate of brandy to turn up.

Eventually, on March 28, Buck discovered, after talking with some of the local Aboriginal people, what he thought was Lasseter's body, along with a set of dentures, in a shallow grave. He then buried him deep in the desert sand. (In 1958, Lasseter was reinterred in the Alice Springs Pioneer Cemetery after his bones were somewhat controversially dug up by the crew for an episode of American TV show *High Adventure*, which was presented by host Lowell Thomas in the 1950s.)

On 29 April 1931, the front page of the *Sydney Mirror* announced: 'LASSETER IS DEAD'. It was the talk of the nation. But when it came to Buck signing a statutory declaration in Sydney, he refused. He was uncertain if the body was actually Lasseter's. According to an account written by John Bailey sixteen years after Lasseter's death, Bob Buck said 'he could not swear whether the skeleton was that of a white or black man'.[5]

Ever suspicious, Blakeley wondered if Buck had assisted Lasseter with his return to America. Some have even claimed that they saw Lasseter on a ship setting sail for the USA; another said that he was spotted in a barber's shop in Pennsylvania; and yet another stated that he saw him wandering the streets in Salt Lake City. Whether it was in relation to the reef or his disappearance, Blakeley blatantly stated in archival footage that Lasseter 'was a liar and a fraud'. From the outset, I believed Lasseter had died in the desert, whether it was through starvation or possible foul play.

Either way, it didn't stop another major expedition for Lasseter's Reef, with the Eclipse Gold Expedition taking place six months after his appalling desert death.

Then, in August of 1931, the second CAGE expedition took place, with Bob Buck engaged as the leader. It seems that as part of Lasseter's original agreement with CAGE, he'd provided the location of the reef on a document written with invisible ink. It was lodged with the Bank of Australasia before departing for the unchartered desert wilderness.

In the event he didn't return from the expedition, the document could be retrieved. When it was, the details Lasseter had left on it appeared inconsistent, so a detective was called in. He revealed a new set of directions, with the coordinates being approximately 23° South latitude and 129° East longitude. These were, as I discovered later, pretty consistent with an article published in the *Daily News* in Perth on 3 August 1948.[6]

At the time, the coordinates were used by Buck and his expedition party, including Western Australian government geologists Henry Talbot and Torrington Blatchford, to guide them to the lost reef. The men visited members of the Pitjantjatjara tribe, given Lasseter had spent his final days with them, and is when Buck is thought to have unearthed Lasseter's fragmented letters buried in the cave floor.

Despite some mixed accounts, as is often the way with Lasseter's Reef, the expedition returned without finding it. Talbot then produced a blistering report, determining that it was impossible for a rich reef of gold to exist in that region.

About a year and a half later, Errol Coote was employed by another company to search for the reef by air from Western Australia. Since Lasseter had previously shared with him what he had seen during the reconnaissance flight in 1930, Coote believed that the reef was to the south of the Rawlinson Ranges. Despite his claims of circling the reef from the air, Coote was unable to land — and the fuel gauge needle was dropping rapidly. He needed to return to base immediately.

Further attempts to raise a ground-based search were ignored. Instead, Coote wrote his book, *Hell's Airport*, in 1934, detailing his version of events with the first CAGE expedition. Although he lost interest in finding it, he firmly believed that the reef existed. So did I.

CHAPTER 4

THE SEARCH BEGINS

Thoughts of Lasseter's Reef swirled through my mind. Hobbling around the house with a walking stick in one hand and the atlas open at the dog-eared page I'd marked in the other, I meticulously scoured the map for clues. Pat would look on and sometimes smile at me quizzically, wondering what new venture I had planned.

The reef had to be out there somewhere. It just wasn't where several other explorers had gone before, that much I did know. But how was I going to get out into the arid heart of Australia, a place where, aside from Aboriginal inhabitants, wildlife and those who knew how to survive the extremes, few had travelled before?

Regardless of whether the reef existed or not, it gave me something other than frustration, sleepless nights and rehabilitating an ankle to focus on.

Although I knew the basis of Lasseter's story, at the time I didn't want to overwhelm or confuse myself with the wide-ranging accounts about him. I was more interested in the geography and the landmarks. How else can you find the needle if you don't find the right haystack?

There were two books that I did read, though. The first one being a later edition of the best-selling *Lasseter's Last Ride*, written by Ion L. Idriess about six months after Lasseter's death, and which, remarkably, has had at least forty reprints since then. Mixing fact with fiction, Idriess acquired — possibly secretly at the time — the various letters penned by Lasseter during the latter stages of the expedition. They were originally found by Bob Buck and then passed on to Lasseter's wife, Rene. This haphazard collection of letters, none of which were dated, is, as mentioned in chapter 3, what eventually became known as Lasseter's Diary. It now forms part of the collection at the Mitchell Library at the State Library of New South Wales.

The other book that caught my attention was Errol Coote's *Hell's Airport*. Based on Coote's recollections of spending time with Lasseter during the CAGE expedition, this is where I found what to look for with the specific landmarks surrounding the approximately 10 mile (16 kilometre) long gold reef, which had ironstone in green slate and a large quartz outcrop. However, Idriess somewhat ambiguously described in his book that 'the yellow stuff was in it thick as plums in a pudding'.[1]

In addition, I would constantly refer to several maps of Australia and more localised ones in and around Central Australia, including acquiring old and new maps, to thoroughly cross-check the areas. It was important to get an understanding of the terrain. Since Lasseter never disclosed the specific location or bearings publically, the landmarks were crucial to finding the reef.

The key landmarks that Lasseter described, based on originally sharing them with Coote during the CAGE expedition and using Lake Christopher in Western Australia as a radial point, included:

1. Three hills that 'could not be mistaken'. To him, they appeared to 'look rather like three women in sun-bonnets talking to one another', which is probably why he referred to them as the 'Three Sisters'.
2. Approximately 35 miles (56 kilometres) to the south-east of the reef was another hill shaped like a 'Quaker hat'. It was tall and conical, appearing to have its 'top cut off'.
3. When looking in a north-westerly direction, along the line of the reef, the Three Sisters appeared to be standing at the end of it.

4. The reef was approximately 10 miles (16 kilometres) to the east of a lakelet, where it was possible to land a plane.
5. The surrounding country was densely timbered and covered with thick mulga, yet the reef could still be viewed from the air.[2]

I was already aware that the reef was approximately 300 miles (482 kilometres) from Alice Springs, therefore placing it near the border of the Northern Territory. Since my focus was to the east, it meant going somewhere towards the tiny, faraway outback town of Boulia in the mostly bone-dry landscape of central-west Queensland.

Overflowing with enthusiasm, I would incessantly chat to just about everyone in Melton, the outer western Melbourne suburb where we were living, about my reference reversal theory with Lasseter's Reef. Some nodded and listened with interest; others politely smiled and said nothing. I could tell they were quietly thinking that I was going crazy. That, or I'd been possessed, possibly by a ghost, perhaps even Lasseter's.

Or was this a sign from the spirit of someone who knew the truth?

The locals were relieved when they found out that I was finally going to the outback, most likely thinking that would be the last time they would hear me speak about Lasseter's Reef.

It took me eleven long years to get out there. During that time, I had to save enough money to buy a suitable vehicle, namely a short-wheelbase Land Rover, along with a trailer, sufficient spare tyres and roof top tent, plus a video camera. Back then, $20,000 was a significant investment. I also had to be in a position to take almost four weeks away from work and family, especially since we had two young children, Daniel and Alycia. At that stage, Pat and I had bought a delicatessen in Melton called the Regional Gourmet Deli. Pat used to work there and the former owner sold it to us. Pat was the backbone of that business. I knew I was asking a lot of her, but she still supported me every step of the way.

In late 1990, less than a year before I left for my outback adventure, Melbourne metallurgist Des Stroud led his third scientific expedition to Central Australia in search of Lasseter's Reef. He was accompanied by a team of geologists, surveyors and prospectors, and had all the latest technological gadgetry. According to a *Sunday Herald Sun* article published on 5 January 1992, Stroud believed the reef had been smothered in sand for years. When he returned from his 1990 expedition, he was confident that his team would uncover the truth that the reef existed. Based on the samples they collected, they just had to narrow it down to one of twenty-five locations, somewhere between the Gibson and Simpson deserts.[3]

Despite Stroud going to what has become known as 'Lasseter Country', and with my intention to go in the completely opposite direction, some people asked me, 'What if he finds it before you do?'

'If he finds it, it means I was wrong. It saves me going out on a trip.'

It wasn't the be-all and end-all for me. Still, nothing conclusive had been found by Stroud and his team. He has since passed away.

In the lead up to my trip, though, I was always planning to travel solo, but Pat and my mum wouldn't hear of it. 'Are you crazy? You can't go out there by yourself,' my mum said anxiously when I first told her. Despite my army training and experience in the oppressively hot and humid jungle of a worn-torn Vietnam, they thought it too risky.

Seeing how concerned they were, and knowing how much finding the reef meant to me, my twenty-one-year-old nephew, Michael Valle, who lived with my parents in the house next door to us, reluctantly volunteered to go with me. When he came over to tell me, I sensed his uncertainty. While staring at the floor pattern in the kitchen and shuffling his long feet, he murmured, 'I'll go with you, Bill.'

Although I'd been somewhat of a father figure to him, I was both surprised and deeply grateful that I didn't have to go on my own. 'Thanks, mate,' I said with my arms outstretched as I went to give him a big bear hug, 'it's extremely courageous of you.'

Michael, a tall, lanky and soft-spoken lad, had never travelled beyond the borders of Victoria. Given his apprehension, I wondered how he'd cope. Then again, neither of us had ever been to the vast expanse of the desert. At the very least, it would be a mind-opening experience.

From then on, I started doing practice runs with Pat and the kids in the four-wheel drive, crawling and jostling over the steep, rocky and deeply rutted trails of the Lerderderg State Park, which is about 94 kilometres north-west of Melbourne. The first time we intended to camp there, but that was short-lived.

We were going carefully up a steep, muddy climb. On the left of the trail was a gaping, water-filled ditch that ran for about 150 metres. Suddenly, the car slid backwards and plunged straight into the cavernous hole. While stuck, I got out and lowered the tyre pressures, then got back in the car to reverse it out. Thank goodness it worked. However, when we drove out, it snapped the exhaust pipe right where the manifold was. The drive home was deafeningly loud.

Besides putting the Land Rover through its paces, I checked and re-checked all the gear almost daily in the months leading up to Michael's and my departure. In addition to the spare tyres and extra fuel, we would have 260 litres of water, backpacks filled with enough food for a week and two-way radios.

I'd marked a number of maps to both take with us and leave with Pat. In the event she didn't hear from us by August 24, she had a copy of the map with the directions we would travel and could send out an alert for a search party to come find us.

The other thing that I took with me on that maiden journey was the page with the key landmarks from *Hell's Airport*. Despite tearing it out of the book almost thirty years ago, and being slightly tattered, it is something I have kept to this day. I also wrote the landmarks down at the time and took them with me, in case I lost the original.

On 3 August 1991, our departure was set: 0300 hours. Like the first CAGE expedition, it seemed logical (and safer) to go to the outback during winter; it was the best time to avoid the harsh desert heat and throng of flies. The main difference was, we were driving from Melton to 300 miles (482 kilometres) east of Alice Springs about two weeks after they'd left there for the west, and it was sixty-one years later.

With the chill air stinging our faces and hands, Michael and I crunched our way across the frost covered lawn to double-check the trailer, then hopped in the Land Rover. Turning on the ignition, the engine purred with a throaty hum. Under the cover of cold darkness, we turned out of the driveway and wended our way through the labyrinth of deserted suburban streets, then picked up the highway to drive towards Ballarat. After a bit of light-hearted banter about finding the legendary gold deposit, there was silence. Michael had fallen asleep.

We weren't even an hour on the road when I noticed an orange flash in the rear view mirror. Puzzled, I thought it was too early for sunrise. Peering into the mirror again, this time I saw bright orange and yellow flames rushing out, licking the rear of the car. 'Shit, we're on fire!' I yelled while nudging Michael with my left arm to rouse him.

Pulling over to the side of the road, I jumped out and raced to the back of the Land Rover. Straight away, I could see the cable from the trailer to the car had shorted, and now it was alight.

Bleary-eyed, Michael stumbled from the car. 'What happened?' he asked, looking on in disbelief.

With no time to answer, let alone get the fire extinguisher, I grabbed the ignited cable with my bare hands. Tearing it off,

I threw it down on the bitumen, attempting to stamp it out. Despite fanning the flames, I persisted until they eventually petered out. Just as well, because there were about 180 litres of diesel fuel stored under the tarp on the trailer.

In the meantime, my hands were covered in melted plastic. I had to wait until later to carefully and almost surgically peel it off. I started to wonder if history was about to repeat itself, especially since the first CAGE expedition was riddled with setbacks.

As the crumbling highway narrowed, we continued towards Adelaide, then had our first overnight stop at the former seaport of Port Augusta, which sits at the head of the Spencer Gulf. The following morning we drove along the straight stretch of line that is the Stuart Highway to Alice Springs. The sun-bleached landscape was filled with contrasting formations and colours, transforming from low undulating hills surrounded by scrubby desert in the south, to the desolate lunar-like-scape and mullock heaps (spoil from opal mines) of Coober Pedy, to the red dirt and flame-coloured mountain ranges with striking bluffs and cliffs flanking the Alice. This sprawling, slower-paced town, which was already a long way from anywhere else, was to be our second port of call before heading deeper into the outback.

As promised, I called Pat that night from the local truck stop. Although it had only been a couple of days since we had left Melton, I missed her and the kids terribly. After we jabbered away for some time, there was a lengthy pause. It was time to say goodbye.

When Pat said, 'Stay safe. I love you,' my pulse jackhammered.

'I love you, too,' I said, before gently hanging up the phone. It would be a while before we spoke again.

The next day, as the bright winter sun beat down on us, Michael and I went to the Alice Springs police station, advising them where we were going. There's no point going out into the desert thinking, 'I'll be right, mate'. That would be foolish. Despite this, a fleeting concern about not returning did enter my mind before Michael and I left, but it was mostly the promise of journeying into the unknown that fuelled me.

Heading slightly north-east from town, the land suddenly opened up to an astonishingly wild, pristine and rugged expanse of rich red earth, cavernous gorges and boundless desert. Taking the turnoff from the Stuart Highway, we headed towards the coarse, ragged and mineral-rich Harts Range. We'd already covered 2500 kilometres and, by my calculations, had about 480 kilometres to go. From this point, I was constantly looking for the landmarks Lasseter had indicated, most notably the 'Three Sisters', and for the city-sized reef to reveal itself.

So far, these three distinctive hills had eluded everyone else, including Lasseter's son Bob who, by this stage, had gone in search of his father's infamous reef at least a dozen times to the west of Central Australia. As for where we were, I was flabbergasted at how similar the landscape was to what Lasseter had described, from flat-topped mountains to smooth, ripple-less waterholes and craggy outcrops. Despite me never having been to this part of Australia before, there was something strangely familiar about it, a sense of returning to the deepest sense of home within. I wanted to savour every moment I could in the desolateness. It was almost transcendental.

For the following days, Michael and I set up camp near a station homestead called The Gardens. There, we got our first taste of the blazing red sun sinking behind the horizon, then heated up tinned baked beans on the flickering campfire. At night, despite the suddenly frigid temperature, we were transfixed by the iridescent shine of the moon and an inky sky pinpricked with gazillions of stars, each one seemingly having its rightful place. Michael quietly wrote in his journal. It became his nightly ritual. He never said much, but I often wondered what he was thinking.

When settling in to sleep on the thin foam mattress in the snug two-person tent on top of the car, we heard dingoes howl in the distance. We kept the rifles close.

In the morning, the sunrise appeared to emerge from the earth with a pinkish-orange and lilac glow that would streak across the vast sky. As the day quickly warmed up, swarms of wild green and yellow budgies would chatter and flutter all around. Their synchronistic wave-like motion was captivating.

From The Gardens, we ventured a little further to the deserted gold mining town of Arltunga, which is about 110 kilometres east of Alice Springs, and almost smack-bang in the middle of Australia. With gold originally found in the creek sands near Paddy's Rockhole in 1887, it was a bit more than a decade later that Arltunga reached its heyday. Initially, the one hundred or so hardworking prospectors would set up their sleeping quarters in tents right next to where they were digging. Besides being struck with gold fever, the constant swinging of cumbersome picks to crack open the thirsty earth was backbreaking work, while the gold panning was long and tiresome.

I was amazed that this little desert town ballooned to 2000 errant miners, and at one stage had a permanent population of about 300. Meanwhile, the heavy equipment for the Government Battery and Cyanide Works that were built there was transported by rail to Oodnadatta. From there, it was hauled on camels and horse-drawn wagons along coaching routes comprising up to 400 miles (643 kilometres) to Alice Springs, then continued on dusty, sandy trails to Arltunga.

To see the town today, it is hard to believe that it was the first major European Settlement in Central Australia. A few bygone buildings remain intact, including the old gaol and police station that was made from stone extracted from the area. There's also a pub, although not operating at the time of writing, and two cemeteries filled with old graves, both marked and unmarked.

Once the gold petered out, the town's population declined to about twenty-five people by 1933. While I admired those fortune hunters who had courageously struggled to dig their way through the hard-baked earth and constantly be covered in a cloud of heavy red dust, little did I know then how Arltunga would play a role in my quest to prove that Lasseter's Reef existed.

CHAPTER 5
REEF REALITY

The rock-strewn four-wheel-drive track to Ruby Gap Nature Park was narrow and bumpy. Located further east of Arltunga, on a dry bed of the Hale River that is filled with large boulders and deep, honey-coloured sand, Ruby Gap was the site of the first mining rush in Central Australia. It was where explorer David Lindsay thought that he'd discovered rubies in the late 1800s. However, it wasn't long after the ruby rush — which is what Lasseter claimed lured him to make his first trip to the desert — that the prospectors discovered the glittering stones weren't rubies at all, they were high-grade garnets. Despite us pulling out the metal detectors and fluidly sweeping them back and forth, there wasn't even a bleep.

The journey from here wasn't as straightforward as I'd anticipated. With rusty barbed-wire fences popping up all over the place, and the track twisting and weaving, we were unable to continue in a straight line to the east as I'd originally planned and marked on the maps. My intention was to follow the Tropic of Capricorn, which has a latitude of approximately 23.26° south of the equator. The idea was that it would give us a start or a direction, especially since this was an area that Lasseter claimed to have travelled through when he was younger, albeit heading in the opposite direction.

Even though we found a promising looking bush track, we got bogged in towering red-orange sand dunes. Several, in fact. After slowly, carefully driving ourselves out of them, we somehow ended up at the Plenty Highway. We were now 60 kilometres out of our way, on the unsealed section, which mostly consisted of thick red dust and sand.

We then made for Atula Station homestead, located on the Plenty River Western Channel. It was our last stop before heading into the remote desert for the Toowoomba Gorge. So far, this would be the most off-road we'd ever gone. I was yet to find out how challenging the terrain would become.

Clumps of spiky golden spinifex grass and grey-green mulga trees with needle-like leaves became so dense, they were more like an impenetrable stronghold. Like the CAGE expedition, we had to repair numerous punctures. In our case, it was both the car tyres and those on the trailer. And then I had to constantly stop to remove the tinder-dry spinifex that gathered in large, prickly tumbleweeds underneath the Land Rover. Dragging them along was becoming an increasing fire hazard.

Wherever we looked, the landscape was rough, parched and hilly. Still, it was important to go at a slow and consistent pace, which meant travelling at an average of 5 kilometres per hour. If you don't tune into the land out there, the desert won't forgive you.

Even the day after leaving the Atula Station homestead, we had to drive along a dry and sandy riverbed — carved in winding snake-like curves — for about 30 kilometres before attempting to cross at the Number Four Bore. After repeated attempts, with wheels spinning and the engine revving, we didn't make it. We drove to the Number Three Bore instead. This time, we were successful.

I started to realise that the number three was becoming prevalent on this trip. Whether it was a sign of some sort, I didn't know. But when it came to departure times, hours travelled, checking my watch or the speedometer, even the fact that we were seeking the three hills, it was a constant recurrence.

As frustrating as it was, it even took us three hours to cross the Plenty River, which had to be done in a couple of sections. From there, we came to a sandy track and headed south. Then we were in first gear all the way; we were now officially in the desert.

Emus took a sticky beak at us as they foraged and strutted through the desert scrub; wild camels sauntered; and majestic wedge-tailed eagles glided and soared across the updrafts and thermals, sometimes swooping and bearing down on prey, including other birds as well as snakes and lizards.

In Australian Aboriginal mythology, Bunjil the eagle is the creator and protector of the land. Symbolically in some other cultures, it is said that eagles represent the freedom and courage to look ahead; to see things from a higher and new perspective, as well as carry the importance of honesty and truthful principles. I marvelled at that thought every time I saw one. That was the very reason I was here: to see myself and the land, as well as find Lasseter's Reef, from a new perspective.

As we followed the course of a meandering creek, I glanced over at Michael. He looked about as deflated as one of our punctured tyres. 'Everything okay?' I asked.

'Yep,' he slowly nodded. 'Do you reckon it's much further to the reef?'

Still wondering where the creek might actually lead us, I said, 'Not long now, mate. We're getting close.' Despite my reassurances, I could tell that he was homesick.

With the sun due to set soon, the glowing red-orange desert sand with a smattering of little ghost gums clinging to the creek bed looked like a good spot to make camp for the night. Sitting in the vastness of this untamed land, sometimes intense loneliness would engulf me. In those moments, my mind would wander to home. How I longed to see Pat's kind smile and soft hazel eyes, as well as hear the kids' playful squeals and cheeky laughter. I also thought of my other two children, Catherine and Anthony, from my first marriage. I often wondered how they were doing. It had been sixteen years since I'd last seen them.

Other times, my mind would be completely thought-free. It had been a long time since my mind had been free of anything. Most of all, I was in awe of how ancient and sacred the infinite desert landscape is.

The next day, after my revelations, Michael and I continued our journey with relative ease. By the afternoon, though, we hit monstrous sand dunes. Suddenly I had visions of the 1930 CAGE expedition digging their vehicles out by shovel and hand. We were okay — until we arrived at the Hay River.

Stranded on the western bank, the sand was loose, thick and crumbly. There was nowhere safe to cross. Thirty minutes later, we found, what I thought was, a lower and more accessible spot, but very quickly we had to stop and unhitch the trailer. Right in front of us, in the middle of the riverbed, was a great big cavernous hole! At some point, it seems torrential rainfall had weighed down heavily on it.

With the trailer now dropped, we had to lug at least half of what was packed in it across a 200-metre stretch and then up a cracked, vertiginous embankment. It took us close to four hours, going back and forth, up and down with twanging muscles. Not surprisingly, Michael struggled. With the sun baking his back, he constantly had to stop, catch his breath, and wipe the sweat dripping from his forehead. Then, miraculously, he would give it his all again.

After that, we did some intense digging with shovels and our bare hands and finally, with a swiftly built pontoon, got the vehicle across and up over the opposite embankment. The rest of our gear, including the fuel, water and spare tyres, was left to gather the following morning. The trailer was going to have to wait a little longer. Overall, it took us two exhaustive days to cross that very short section of the river. In some ways, it was like conquering our own Mount Everest.

While we camped there, on the first evening as we settled down to sleep, we heard a low-pitched roar or whirling sound. At first, we thought it was coming from a didgeridoo. We were too knackered to take much notice, but it was haunting.

Shuddering, Michael whispered, 'I'm scared. I think someone is watching us.'

He was right. The following morning, I found bare human footprints stamped in the powdery earth across the river, near where we had left the trailer.

It was a few years later, when I was speaking with TV presenter Ernie Dingo from *The Great Outdoors* travel show, that I recalled our eerie experience. He told me that Michael and I had most likely heard a bullroarer, an ancient musical instrument or device traditionally used to communicate or send warnings over great distances. In our case, it was probably warning us to get the hell out.

I also realised that where we had crossed the Hay River was not far from where Australian explorer and geologist Cecil Madigan had gone in 1939. This was when his scientific exploration, consisting of nine men and nineteen camels, made its way from Andado Station in the Northern Territory to Birdsville in Queensland. Although Madigan wasn't the first European to officially cross the arid heart, an aerial survey that he went on before his expedition took place saw the region become recognised as the Simpson Desert. It was named in honour of the expedition's sponsor, Allen Simpson, the former president of the South Australian branch of the Royal Geographical Society of Australasia.[1]

Before we could leave the Hay River, we needed to get the trailer across. As Michael heaved the trailer, I lifted the back and placed a piece of wood underneath. With all my strength, I pushed it forward to the area we needed to cross. Using planks of wood, we then created an 8-foot-long track, like a corduroy, constantly having to relay a piece at a time whenever we got to the end of it. About halfway along the riverbed, we tied some rope to one end of the trailer and secured the other end to the Land Rover. For the next two hours, we gradually pulled the trailer across. Then we had to reload it.

After that exasperating and bone-tiring effort, Michael and I spent the best part of the day travelling to another and smaller river crossing in the Adam Range. Despite the seemingly endless sandhills and ridgelines, and only getting bogged twice, we made it to what became our next overnight camp site. While there, we decided to do some metal detecting. Although there were lots of promising looking rocks with golden flecks on the ground, when scraping the flecks off, they disintegrated. Turns out that they were thin shards of mica.

By this stage of our trip, I realised that we'd travelled 200 kilometres more than I'd anticipated. It was more like 402 miles, not 300 miles from Alice Springs. Had we missed our mark? We were, after all, on day ten of our journey. All I did know is that we had to continue east.

After bouncing our way up, down and across some of the most inhospitable country in the Land Rover, to our amazement, we suddenly arrived at a smooth, flat clearing. We stopped to inhale the rich earth, the green trees and the cerulean sky, then Michael had a crack at repairing his first tyre puncture. Having helped me so many times now, it was terrific to see him take the initiative to fix things or try something new, especially in such a stark and foreign environment. Not only had his confidence and sense of independence grown, he'd officially transitioned into manhood.

At the same time, we discovered that two of the jerry cans with water had been punctured. Forty litres of water had evaporated into nothingness. Although we had a reserve, and having taken a slight detour, I hoped that we had enough left. Since leaving the highway, it had been a painstakingly slow journey.

From here, we bumped around a bit and came across an area with glistening white quartz scattered all through it. This was exactly the kind of country Lasseter had described. We must be getting close, I thought. A bit further on, there was a giant quartz blow. Even better, it was 'peeping' through the mulga.

My heart erupted with elation while my stomach somersaulted. I stopped the car and Michael and I got out quickly to have a closer look. Walking towards the blow, Michael's eyes widened as he pointed to the distance and exclaimed, 'Look over there!'

There they were: three hills, standing with full, rounded bases that had distinctive rims and were crowned with small, angular peaks, in the middle of absolutely nowhere. On the one hand, they appeared to be breast-shaped hills. On the other hand, they looked like three women talking side-by-side. Although Lasseter had described these three hills, or Three Sisters, as wearing 'sun-bonnets', to me they looked more like they were wearing bell-shaped dresses, as was done in the nineteenth century. (That's probably due to them having endured more than one hundred years of erosion.) There was no way that these hills could EVER be mistaken.

Relief and joy surged through me. Still, I needed to be one hundred percent sure. I grabbed the maps to go over the distances, again and again. Between looking through binoculars to scan the landscape and glancing back to the maps, they were spot on. This was exactly where I'd marked the map when I watched *The Legend of Lasseter* documentary eleven years prior: 300 miles (482 kilometres) east of Alice Springs!

Incredibly, and according to what Coote had described in his book, we already had about half of the landmarks: the three hills, the prolific mulga and a Quaker hat. What's more, all of these landmarks could be seen from the west, which is *exactly* the direction Michael and I had just come from. And it was the direction that Lasseter had indicated was the only way to clearly see them.

My euphoric state, however, took us in another unanticipated direction. My intention was to drive the Land Rover around the area to get a closer look, especially since it was about 35 miles (56 kilometres) to the Quaker hat. Somehow, we ended up driving away from the area. Before long, we were back at the Donohue Highway — and on our way to Boulia!

While driving along the narrow dirt road, disappointment sunk down my throat, then crept into my stomach. Thumping the steering wheel hard, I shook my head and groaned to myself, 'For God's sake, Bill. What are you doing? Focus.'

The logical side of me knew that we should have first walked the area, especially to go atop the three hills from where we could take bearings and get a clearer perspective. Perhaps I had a touch of gold fever.

While I briefly thought about turning the vehicle around, given we'd just crossed some immensely rugged country, and having slightly less water, I wasn't going back into the desert at that moment. If we did, we'd be asking for trouble, even though we'd just found Lasseter's Reef.

It was just after three a.m. the following morning when we arrived in Boulia. Sitting on the edge of the vast desert and surrounded by sheep and cattle country, this was to be our pit stop for three days.

Wandering around the wide streetscapes in daylight, the small, dusty town is filled with a mix of new and old buildings, along with affable locals who have plenty of time for a yarn. It also happened to be where Burke and Wills passed through in 1861, with the local waterway subsequently named the Burke River. For years, the quiet town has been more commonly known for its strange spectral light: the Min Min, which some Aboriginal people believe is the spirits of the elders appearing in the night.

I phoned Pat to tell her our extraordinary news. She was just as excited as we were, although I think she was more relieved that we'd survived to share the story.

While in Boulia, Michael and I restocked with essentials and refuelled, and got some much needed rest. We also discussed how we would return to the reef to take more photos, as well as collect rock samples from the top of it. We agreed that these would further prove that Lasseter's Reef existed.

However, when it came to departing Boulia and heading down the Donohue Highway in the direction of the reef, my enthusiasm waned. It quickly turned to unease. For the life of me, I couldn't understand why. What Michael and I had discovered would rewrite Australian history books.

About to turn off the highway again, at a crossroad, I turned to Michael and noticed how glum he looked. Watching his chin drop down further and his shoulders slump, I asked him, 'Would you rather go back to the reef, or go home?'

'I'll go to the reef, because finding it has been your dream for years,' he mumbled, looking down at the floor.

I paused, took a deep breath and asked him again, 'But what do you really want to do?'

'I want to go home.'

Fortunately, we did come home. When we returned, I was cleaning the Land Rover and underneath it I noticed that the wire for the lights had been stripped; it was sitting flush beneath the fuel tank. Had we gone across that jagged desert terrain for a second time, I doubt that it, or us, would have lasted. It would have been kaboom, not eureka.

CHAPTER 6
DIGGING DEEPER

I was stoked to have found the reef and be back home with Pat and the kids, but I wasn't myself. Nor was Michael. On the one hand, spending a few weeks in the solitude of the sunbaked outback heightened our senses. From morning to night, the stark beauty of the universe was constantly reflected back to us through the ever-changing landscape. We were deeply present out there. On the other hand, coming home to familiar surrounds — to civilisation — weighed us down. Even watching TV, I was disconnected. It was like picking up on a negative frequency.

From the moment we pulled in for fuel at Coober Pedy on the return trip, the comedown was already kicking in. It was a startling contrast, given it was only a few weeks beforehand that we'd stopped there, in awe of the journey we were embarking on. This time, though, we couldn't get out of there fast enough, and it only intensified as we continued to Melbourne.

For the first two weeks after being back, I hardly spoke. Normally I talk non-stop. Pat and those who know me well kept asking, 'Everything alright, Bill? You're awfully quiet.'

'I'm fine,' I'd reply. I guess I was hovering between an integration and transition phase, occasionally uttering profound revelations, from the importance of listening to nature's wisdom to everything having a life force.

At the very least, I began to understand why Aboriginal people have such a strong spiritual connection to the land. We are all here as it custodians. Nonetheless, I briefly earnt the nickname of Reverend Bill. I also started to wonder if my quietude was a case of post-camping depression.

After grounding myself, I returned to the deli with renewed vigour. All around, I put up the photos of the trip to Lasseter's Reef, especially of the three hills and the quartz blow, willing to chat with everyone who came in and was interested to find out more about it. 'Have you heard about Lasseter's Reef?' I would ask them fervently. In order to get back out there and take samples, it required financial backing to engage a mining company.

I also had a lot more research to do. Although I'd found the reef, I still wanted to disprove myself. That meant poring over everything I could — as baffling and inconsistent as it was — about Lasseter.

As for his early life, he was born on 27 September 1880 at Bamganie, near Meredith in Victoria, and given the name of Lewis Hubert Lasseter. He had three siblings, namely older brother Arthur, his sister Lillian and younger brother Claude, who died from consumption (tuberculosis) when he was about sixteen years old.[1] Lasseter's mother died when he and his siblings were quite young, while his English-born father, who didn't seem to think much of his second son, was often away working as a labourer and eventually remarried. Inevitably, it led to an unhappy and troubled childhood, with Lasseter running away from home by about age ten.

For a while, he lived with a well-off family in Colac. During that time, he did odd jobs, including working as an office boy at the local newspaper, presumably the *Colac Herald*.[2] However, in September and October of 1896, I was surprised to learn that Lasseter was in the newspaper for other reasons. The *Colac Herald* reported that he had been arrested and charged for an armed robbery at a local emporium.[3] He was then sentenced to the Pakenham Reformatory for boys for two years.

In his fascinating and meticulously researched book *The Search for Harold Lasseter*, journalist Murray Hubbard reproduces a document from the reformatory's register stating that Lasseter was admitted there in October 1896 and then absconded one year later. Interestingly, the remarks in that same document say that a young Lasseter was prone to being 'untruthful'.[4]

Given 1897 is the year Lasseter, predominantly, claimed to have crossed the continent and found his gold reef, I started to wonder how a seventeen-year-old lad, who had never been in the desert before, could have achieved that in such a short timeframe. If he had absconded from the reformatory in October, that would have given him less than two and a half months to travel from east to west. Since he journeyed there in the latter stage of the year, he would have endured searing heat. He would have had to carry an ample water supply, as well as food, just to get from Cairns to Central Australia, plus he was travelling solo on horseback. What's more, he had to sail on a ship from Melbourne to Cairns to get there in the first place.

Something else that occurred to me was, where did he get the horses from, and how did he acquire them? Perhaps old habits were put to use, because it is unlikely that he had the money to buy them at that young stage of his life. Even if he didn't steal the horses, he would have had to have worked for at least a couple of months to acquire them. So if the theory that he may have worked on trawlers in Cairns was true, he still wouldn't have had sufficient time to travel across the desert. The timing didn't add up.

Also documented in *The Search for Harold Lasseter* was some correspondence Lasseter's sister Lillian McGrath (her married name) had with her nephew Bob Lasseter, who has spent the best part of his life piecing together his father's story. Lillian indicated that she received a letter from her brother while he was at the reformatory. Apparently, Lasseter was miserable there, so she helped him get back home after he'd absconded.[5]

What intrigued me most about this correspondence was that, according to Lillian, the seventeen-year-old Lasseter landed a job on a coastal boat and then sailed to England. A couple of letters were exchanged, but then she heard nothing for at least two years. When she did hear from him again, the letter had been sent from America. Lasseter attributed the lack of correspondence due to ill health and memory loss. It turns out that having brain fog was a frequent occurrence for him over the years.[6]

Reinforcing that Lasseter couldn't have been in the central Australian desert in 1897, Murray Hubbard includes an enlistment form for when Lasseter enlisted in the army in Melbourne in 1916. It shows that Lasseter had been with the Royal Navy for four years, until he was discharged in 1901.[7] That meant he would have joined the navy in late 1897. Yet Lasseter told John Bailey and Fred Blakeley before the CAGE expedition commenced that he crossed the centre of Australia in 1897, worked in the Western Australian goldfields for a few years, then went back to relocate the reef with Harding in 1900.

To further add to the inconsistencies, a letter written by Lasseter to Bailey on 1 April 1930 indicated that he had known of this ginormous lode at the western end of the MacDonnell Ranges for the past thirty years. If that was the case, it would have been 1900, not 1897, that he first found it. Either way, he couldn't have been there. He was in the navy, wasn't he?[8]

As for Lasseter's time overseas, after England he possibly visited France, then Belgium. There were even claims that he worked at a Belfast shipyard in Ireland.

Although it was thought that Lasseter was in America from about 1901 and definitely until late 1909, I discovered that he was actually there since at least 1900. Thanks to a friend of mine, he unearthed the following signed copy of Lasseter's Declaration of Intention when applying for

American citizenship with the Bureau of Immigration and Naturalization.

Dated 17 December 1907, we can see that Lasseter declared that he arrived in Baltimore, Maryland, 'on or about the 15 September 1900'.[9] He also stated that he immigrated to the US from Glasgow, Scotland, on the *Inkum* vessel.

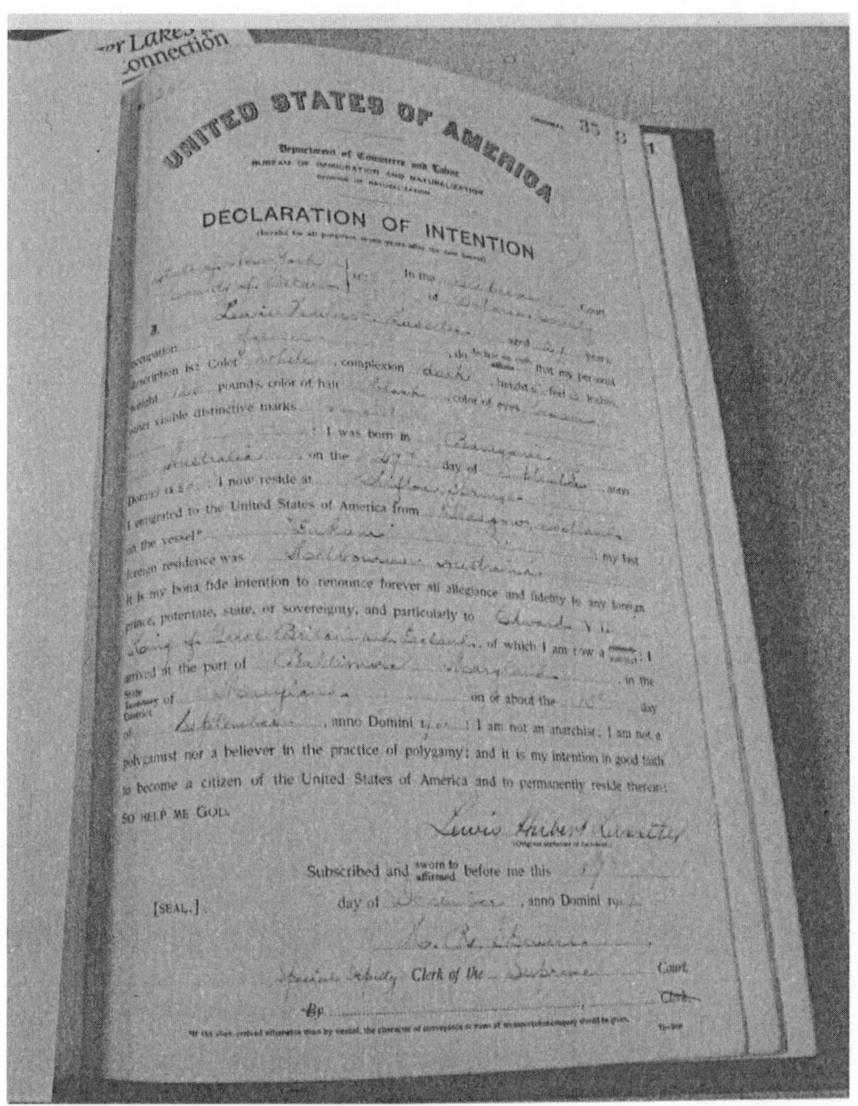

UNITED STATES OF AMERICA

Department of Commerce and Labor

Bureau of Immigration and Naturalization

Division of Naturalization

DECLARATION OF INTENTION

In the ... Court

I, Lewis Hubert Lasseter, aged ... years, occupation ..., do declare on oath that my personal description is: Color white, complexion dark, height ... feet ... inches, weight ... pounds, color of hair black, color of eyes ..., other visible distinctive marks ...

I was born in ... Australia, on the 27th day of September anno Domini ...; I now reside at Clifton Springs ...

I emigrated to the United States of America from Glasgow, Scotland on the vessel* Inkum; my last foreign residence was ... Australia.

It is my bona fide intention to renounce forever all allegiance and fidelity to any foreign prince, potentate, state, or sovereignty, and particularly to Edward VII, King of Great Britain and Ireland, of which I am now a subject; I arrived at the port of Baltimore, Maryland, in the State of Maryland, on or about the 15 day of September, anno Domini 1900; I am not an anarchist; I am not a polygamist nor a believer in the practice of polygamy; and it is my intention in good faith to become a citizen of the United States of America and to permanently reside therein: SO HELP ME GOD.

Lewis Hubert Lasseter
(Original signature of declarant.)

Subscribed and sworn to before me this 17 day of December, anno Domini 19..

[SEAL.]

Special Deputy Clerk of the Supreme Court.

By ...

*If the alien arrived otherwise than by vessel, the character of conveyance or name of transportation company should be given.

Lewis Hubert Lasseter's Declaration of Intention, United States of America, 1907.

UNITED STATES OF AMERICA

Department Of Commerce And Labor
BUREAU OF IMMIGRATION AND NATURALIZATION
DIVISION OF NATURALIZATION

DECLARATION OF INTENTION

(Invalid for all purposes seven years after the date hereof)

State of New York, County of Ontario. In the Supreme Court of Ontario County;

I, Lewis Hubert Lasseter aged 27 years, occupation farmer, do declare on oath that my personal description is: Color White, Complexion Dark, Height 5 feet 3 inches, Weight 125 pounds, Color of hair Black, Color of eyes Brown, other visible distinctive marks None.

I was born in Bamganie Australia, on the 27th day of September, anno Domini 1880; I now reside at Clifton Springs.

I emigrated to the United States of America from Glasgow Scotland on the vessel Inkum; my last foreign residence was Melbourne Australia.

It is my bona fide intention to renounce forever all allegiance and fidelity to any foreign prince, potentate, state, or sovereignty, and particularly to Edward VII King of Great Britain and Ireland, of which I am now a subject; I arrived at the port of Baltimore Maryland in the state of Maryland on or about the 15th day of September, anno Domini 1900; I am not an anarchist; I am not a polygamist, nor a believer in the practice of polygamy; and it is my intention in good faith to become a citizen of the United States of America and to permanently reside therein; SO HELP ME GOD.

Lewis Hubert Lasseter
(Original Signature of Declarant)

Subscribed and sworn to before me this 17th day of December, anno Domini 1907
Special Deputy Clerk of the Supreme Court

But, according to the Caledonian Maritime Research Trust, which has an extensive database about Scottish-built ships, the *Inkum*, a general cargo steamer built by Alexander Stephens and Sons Ltd., wasn't launched until 19 June 1901.[10] Besides, its first port of register was Liverpool in north-west England. Perhaps Lasseter helped with the construction of the *Inkum*, but there's no way he could have sailed to America on it when he said he did.

There is the possibility that Lasseter arrived in America even earlier based on his letter to the editor of the *Tenterfield Star*. Published on 1 June 1915, it stated that he was in America for twelve years.[11] That would mean he was there as of 1898. Regardless of when he arrived in the good ol' U.S. of A., as I said in chapter 1, that is where he met and married his first wife, Florence Scott. But what I didn't realise was, three years after their daughter Ruby was born, they had a son, Arthur. He died nine days after he was born.

While in America, Lasseter is thought to have completed various correspondence courses, including agriculture, navigation and compass surveying.[12] Despite the certificates reflecting these qualifications, it appears to me, and as some handwriting experts have argued over the years, that Lasseter may have signed at least one of them in his own hand.

After Florence's mother died, they sold her family property and came to Australia, with Lasseter and his family appearing on the doorstep of his sister's and her husband's house at West Street, Evandale, in Adelaide. Within a few weeks, the family of three were off to start a new life in rural New South Wales.[13]

Moving to a small lease-hold farm near Tabulam, Lasseter, his wife and daughter Ruby, along with second daughter Beulah who was born in 1911 and was called Bill by her father, lived there until 1915. During that time Lasseter worked as a road maintenance man with the local council. He also had a regular column, "Tabulam Tinklings", which appeared in the *Tenterfield Star*.

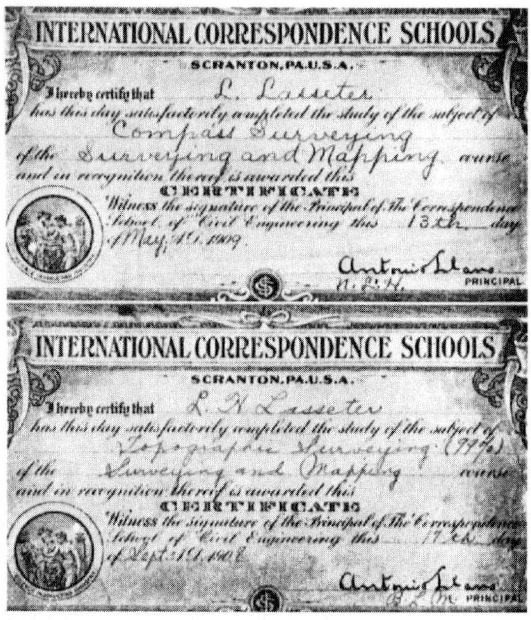

INTERNATIONAL CORRESPONDENCE SCHOOLS

SCRANTON, PA. U.S.A.

I hereby certify that L. Lasseter has this day satisfactorily completed the study of the subject of Compass Surveying of the Surveying and Mapping course and in recognition thereof is awarded this

CERTIFICATE

Witness the signature of the Principal of The Correspondence School of Civil Engineering this 13th day of May A.D. 1909.

PRINCIPAL

INTERNATIONAL CORRESPONDENCE SCHOOLS

SCRANTON, PA. U.S.A.

I hereby certify that L. H. Lasseter has this day satisfactorily completed the study of the subject of Topographic Surveying (97%) of the Surveying and Mapping course and in recognition thereof is awarded this

CERTIFICATE

Witness the signature of the Principal of The Correspondence School of Civil Engineering this 17th day of Sept. A.D. 1908.

PRINCIPAL

The compass surveying and topographic surveying certificates that Lasseter claimed to have obtained while he was living in America. (Mitchell Library, State Library of NSW)

Now given Lasseter was in Tabulam until 1915, when he first wrote to politician Albert E. "Texas" Green with his letter dated 14 October 1929, he claimed that he found his fabulously rich gold reef eighteen years prior, making it 1911.[14] How could he have done that if he was still in northern New South Wales? Perhaps he confused it with his second daughter's year of birth.

Add to that how Errol Coote recalls in his book *Hell's Airport* that Lasseter claimed in front of him at the AWU office that he managed to get a handful of men together to attempt to relocate the reef from Central Australia in 1911:

> We started inland from Oodnadatta, but they expected to find station homesteads every day or so, and finding none, decided to turn back. Anyhow, their booze had given out, and they wanted to get back to the Transcontinental Hotel at Oodnadatta. I fell off the camel on the return trip and was

> slightly injured. I have often tried to get an expedition to go out there, but nobody seems to want to tackle the job.[15]

Aside from Lasseter getting his dates mixed up, I now realised that his story about finding the reef, let alone relocating it, didn't gel.

One thing is certain, though: Lasseter's creativity was in full swing while in Tabulam. In 1913, and before the Sydney Harbour Bridge was commissioned for construction, he'd drawn a design for a single-span arch bridge to extend across Sydney Harbour.[16] Whether he actually submitted it or not at the time isn't known. While there are similarities with Lasseter's drawing, obviously chief engineer John Bradfield came to be known as the bridge's designer.

The following year, Lasseter submitted a somewhat intriguing letter to the American *Phelps Citizen* newspaper, this time discussing his investment in a gold mine. Dated 19 May 1914, he wrote:

> There has been a revival in the mining industry here lately owing to some big finds of molybdenite; one lucky man got $600 worth in one day; it wasn't me tho' I recently invested in a gold mine, hoping to make a pot of money. Well I got a pot of experience instead. If I keep on I will soon have a million dollars' worth of experience; it will never reach gar tho' if placed on the market.[17]

Although Lasseter hadn't declared his find about a gold reef when he wrote this, why would he invest in a gold mine when he's supposedly found a fabulously rich gold-bearing reef, whether it was back in 1897, 1900 or 1911? I was constantly surprised by the anomalies.

Gold mining investments aside, in 1915 Lasseter lodged a provisional specification for a patent disc plough, but it didn't generate any interest.

After the outbreak of World War I, it was in 1916 that Lasseter and his family moved to Melbourne where he unsuccessfully attempted to enlist in the army. According to his attestation paper, at 5 feet 2 inches tall (158 centimetres), he was too short to be recruited.[18] At the time, they had increased the minimum height requirements. Eighteen days later, he again applied as a 'bridge engineer' and was enlisted in the Australian Imperial Force. Perhaps noting that he was 5 feet 3 inches (161 centimetres) on this application and travelling to Neerim Junction, north of Warragul, in the early hours of the morning, when our bodies are typically a tad taller, made the difference.

While based at Seymour, Lasseter went AWOL not once, but twice. The first time was for fifty-nine hours. He was subsequently confined to the barracks for seven days. In this case, though, he was confined at the Langwarrin Camp, specifically its Venereal Diseases Hospital. The next time Lasseter upped the ante and went AWOL for seven days, which earnt him fourteen days in the barracks at Seymour. After nine months of 'service', he was discharged for being medically unfit.[19] His record stated that he was blind in his right eye from an injury sustained six years earlier.[20] How did he pass the medical examination in the first place?

Then, in November of that year, it is thought that Lasseter may have placed his own death notice in the *Sydney Mail*, saying he had 'died of wounds' suffered at Gallipoli. However, he'd never been there.[21] Was this strange hoax Lasseter's doing to escape an unfulfilling first marriage, or to get out of debt? He was struggling financially. Or did the newspaper make a grave error? Either way, the *Sydney Mail* corrected the mistake a couple of weeks later. Lasseter was alive and living with his family in Victoria.

With work becoming sporadic, and urgently in need of a pay cheque, Lasseter left his family and spent much of 1917 in South Australia. He even briefly worked on the wharves of Fremantle in Western Australia.[22]

In August that year, back in Adelaide, he reenlisted with the army. But that barely lasted a couple of months. On 11 September 1917, Lasseter was admitted to the 7th Australian General Hospital at Keswick in an unconscious state and with a scalp wound. He'd inadvertently got involved in a street brawl, so he claimed.

Although his army medical record states, based on the dates in the admission and discharge columns, that he was in that hospital for about four weeks, in another column on the exact same page it says that he only stayed there for seven days. After that, he was transferred to the No.17 Australian Auxiliary Hospital at Torrens Park, where he stayed for six days. Despite his recovery and being given the all clear, in November he was declared medically unfit for duty.[23] This time his medical record declared him as being 'mentally deficient' and noted that he had 'marked hallucinations'. It also stated that he 'wants to join the Flying Corps as a friend is going to present him with an aeroplane'.[24]

Originally I thought, as did Murray Hubbard, that Lasseter had stayed in the Adelaide Hospital (now known as the Royal Adelaide Hospital), then the Adelaide Army Hospital, largely due to the abbreviated and somewhat ambiguous hospital names on his army medical forms. The point is, he *had* been hospitalised in Adelaide.

There was something else that caught my attention on Lasseter's attestation paper for enlisted members of service — his address. It showed that he'd nominated his permanent address as 'c/o Thoms Commercial Road, Port Adelaide'.[25] Back then, this lively portside strip was known for its public houses, otherwise known as licensed hotels and inns. It seems that Lasseter was staying at a boarding house there. I also wondered if Lasseter had visited his sister Lillian, given she lived in Adelaide.

After contacting the State Library of South Australia, I discovered that in 1917 Lillian lived at 66 Harrow Road in College Park, a suburb just down the road from Evandale, where she was previously residing.[26] While there's no known correspondence between her and Lasseter, it is possible that during his time in Adelaide, he would stop at her house on occasion. He may have even stayed with her to convalesce before returning to Melbourne.

Unlike many other lines of enquiry made over the years, I soon realised that Lasseter being in Adelaide in 1917 would be a pivotal year with his story about the reef, which I elaborate on in later chapters. Besides, I had so many piles of documents, files and books about Lasseter and the CAGE expedition, along with maps and photos of the reef, they were starting to spill over from the billiard table and spread all throughout the living room.

Back in Melbourne by early 1918, Lasseter made a pension application, didn't show up for his scheduled appointment in March, then by the middle of the year moved with his family to Toora in South Gippsland.[27] This is yet another year, and a different story, that he refers to down the track as being a time when he returned to the find reef from Oodnadatta.[28] According to Lasseter, this particular expedition took place thanks to Hans Erickson, a camel driver who gave the directive to go towards Alice Springs. Again, he never got there.

While in Toora, Lasseter repaired navigational beacons in Corner Inlet's channel, on a work boat called *Victory*, which is now proudly displayed at the nearby Foster Museum. However, at the time, he was struggling to provide for himself and his family, especially since he'd lost all of their savings. He was known, especially to his wife Florence and their two daughters, to frequent Melbourne and squander what little money they had on his lady friends.

As always, Lasseter came up with novel ideas, including establishing a shipbuilding yard at Port Welshpool.[29] He also proposed the creation of an industrial-type town for returned soldiers. Neither of them came to fruition.

By 1920, Lasseter and his family were living at Foster, where he proposed a hydro-electric scheme at Agnes Falls.

While it had merit, these were tough economic times — it was the post-war period.

In *The Search for Harold Lasseter*, Lasseter's daughter Beulah recalls how she and her sister Ruby would listen to their father regale about the reef and play with some gold nuggets in their home at Foster.[30] Since I'd now come to realise that Lasseter couldn't have found the reef, where did these nuggets come from?

As for Lasseter's sister Lillian, she was equally puzzled about his knowledge of the reef. In another of her reproduced letters, she too questions how or when the reef could have been discovered. According to Lillian, neither she nor their father had ever heard Lasseter speak of it beforehand.[31]

Sometime in 1921, Lasseter, his first wife and two daughters were living in Melbourne's bayside suburbs, but the ever-restless Lasseter was rarely at home with his family. During Melbourne Cup week of that same year, he went to the races, backed the favourite and lost all of his money. According to Beulah, who'd picked the winner, he returned home without saying a word. It was the last time that she saw her father.[32]

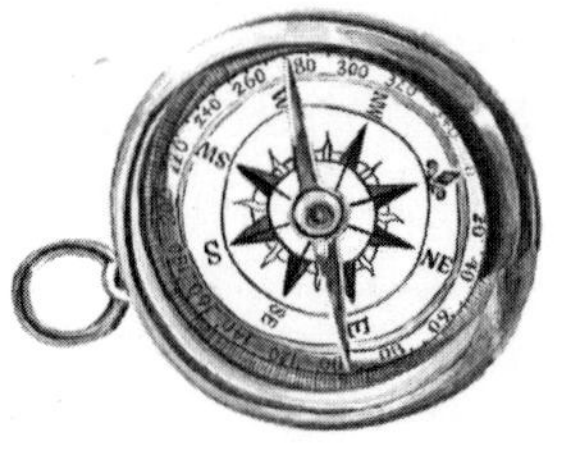

CHAPTER 7

CONSISTENT DISCREPANCIES

Lasseter has been called many things both during his life and after his death, but clearly he was an eccentric and tragic genius with grand, hopeful visions. As Murray Hubbard aptly concluded in his book, Lasseter craved recognition, yet it was always frustratingly out of his grasp.[1] It was as if he was struggling to hold on to a slippery fish. Besides enduring a difficult childhood, this was a man who bore emotional and physical scars. He also copped a few serious knocks to the head in adulthood.

At some point, Lasseter had a steel plate inserted in his skull, possibly at the Caulfield Repatriation Hospital. It is also possible that he married a nurse who worked there.[2] If he did, like me, his second marriage didn't last long. (Mine only lasted two months.)

Then, in 1924, Lasseter married Rene, also a nurse, although in this instance it is believed that they first met on a train. It was also when he changed his name from Lewis Hubert Lasseter to Harold Bell Lasseter. Perhaps, as some say, he was inspired by America's best-selling author Harold Bell Wright, given his popular novel and photoplay *The Mine with the Iron Door* was published the year prior. It was, after all, a romantic tale revolving around the discovery of a mother lode.

Another book that may have inspired the name change was Simpson Newland's *Blood Tracks of the Bush*. Published in 1900, it too had a theme of finding an inland El Dorado.

As for Lasseter, he was still married to his first two wives, and plunging further into a debt spiral.

Not long after marrying for a third time, Lasseter and his new wife moved to Kogarah in New South Wales. Soon after, he moved to Canberra to work on the new Parliament House, with Rene, a young Bob and baby Betty joining him towards the end of 1926. While working as a carpenter there, he would beguile others with his well-worn yarn of how he'd found a fabulously rich gold reef in Central Australia, even pointing it out on a map. Lasseter's lust for gold saw him concoct a hoax for the workers at the Mount Ainslie camp, where he claimed to have found bucket loads of gold dust in the creek. As it turned out, the gold was nothing more than brass filings.[3]

After his two-year stint in Canberra, Lasseter returned to Sydney and began, somewhat ironically, working on the construction of the Sydney Harbour Bridge, from which he was then dismissed. It was while he was working at the pottery at Redfern that he also built his home at Kogarah, with its

Lasseter with wife Rene and son Bob in about 1925, prior to him relocating to Canberra where he worked as a carpenter, including some time building what is now known as the old Parliament House. (State Library of South Australia B 53583)

concrete foundations reinforced by tramway rails. There's no doubt that Lasseter was quite the innovator.

In September of 1929, he had a letter published in *Australian Shipping and Steel and The Harbour*. This was when Lasseter was seeking both recognition and compensation, having claimed to have submitted the original design for the Sydney Harbour Bridge and it being plagiarised.[4] Although he did actually draw an impressive design back in 1913 complete with horse-drawn carriages, which his son Bob Lasseter has had in his possession, it didn't make any difference. Was it a case of desperate times calling for desperate measures?

By the beginning of 1930, it certainly seems so. In view of the Western Australian government not pursuing Lasseter's claim of finding a rich gold seam, he was expecting the bailiff to arrive on his doorstep at any moment. He placed an ad in the *Sydney Morning Herald* seeking £150 equity in his 'new brick cottage' at Kogarah. With no takers, he repeated the ad a couple more times, although upped the size of the loan in the last one. In between time, he wrote to the Japanese Consulate indicating that he had some top secret information that required the Japanese Emperor's urgent attention.[5] Although the exact details of the letter are unknown, he never received a reply.

Yet it wasn't even four years beforehand that Lasseter had written to a Mr Honeysett, the social service officer at the Canberra Capital Commission, to vent his frustration about the brutality of war and warn about the possibility of Japan invading Australia.[6] His prediction was spot-on, but he was about sixteen years too early.

Once CAGE was established in 1930, things *appeared* to be looking up for Lasseter. Finally, someone was willing to back one of his ideas, and an extraordinary one at that. However, it wasn't long before the inconsistencies, along with his 'jumbled moods' as Fred Blakeley described in his posthumously published book *Dream Millions* (which had a revised edition,

Lasseter's Dream of Millions, in 1984), continued to reveal themselves.

Even on the agreement that Lasseter made with John Bailey in June 1930, which wasn't disclosed until Kathryn England's book *Lasseter: the man, the legend, the gold* was published in 2003, the year on the document states that he was searching for rubies and subsequently discovered the reef in 1894.[7] That meant he would have been thirteen or fourteen years old.

Something else that caught my attention was the initial interest from John Bailey to include the accomplished and remarkably well-connected RAF pilot Charles Lexius-Burlington, who promptly helped to arrange for the Thornycroft truck to be used as part of the 1930 CAGE expedition. However, it seems he was considered to be more of a threat when expressing interest in being a part of the whole event as mechanic.

Aside from Coote voicing his disapproval about his involvement, or more likely being intimidated by Lexius-Burlington's flawless service record, Lasseter threatened to withdraw from the expedition. Not only did Lexius-Burlington know the ins and outs of aircraft, he had worked with gold-mining companies in far-flung parts of New Guinea. He was also well-versed in reading maps.[8]

You would think these attributes would be a distinct advantage when looking to relocate a gold reef that has an estimated worth of £66 million in the arid heart of Australia. But if Lasseter walked, so did his knowledge of the distinctive landmarks, and that was a risk CAGE wasn't willing to take. In turn, Lexius-Burlington was ousted and Phil Taylor was then engaged as mechanic.

Even when it came to the CAGE expedition members arriving in Alice Springs, the locals were curious about the forty-nine-year-old Lasseter claiming to have found a gold reef about thirty-two years prior, let alone having ever visited the outback before. In his book *Lasseter's Dream of Millions*, Fred

A G R E E M E N T made this *fourteenth* day of *June*
in the year One thousand nine hundred and thirty BETWEEN
JOHN BAILEY of 321 Pitt Street Sydney on behalf of the Company below mentioned which Company is hereinafter referred to
as "The Company" of the one part A N D LEWIS HAROLD BELL
LASSITER of Orient Road Kogarah hereinafter called the said
Lassiter of the other part WHEREAS the said Lassiter claims
to know the whereabouts of a gold-bearing reef in Central
or Western Australia AND WHEREAS the said Lassiter in the
year 1894 was searching for rubies in the McDonald Ranges and
after proceeding therefrom in a certain direction came upon
the said gold-bearing reef of stone and chipped off a bag of
samples therefrom AND WHEREAS the said Lassiter traced the
said reef for over a quarter of a mile finding it carried
gold all the way AND WHEREAS three years later the said
Lassiter accompanied by a surveyor rediscovered the said reef
and traced it for ten miles or thereabouts and the average
assay of the whole length of the said reef of ten miles or
thereabouts revealed over three ounces of gold to the ton
AND WHEREAS the said Lassiter has disclosed certain particulars to two meetings of certain proposed shareholders of
the Company hereinafter mentioned and has agreed to guide a
party of prospectors to the location of the said reef AND
WHEREAS the said Lassiter states that he has not disclosed
to anyone the exact location of the said reef AND WHEREAS he
has stated that he has not entered into any other legal
agreement with any other person or persons or corporation
other than and except the Agreement herein contained AND
WHEREAS the Company to be called Central Australian Gold
Exploration Company Limited is about to be formed under the
provisions of the Companies Acts of New South Wales with a
nominal capital of Five thousand pounds (£5000) divided into
five thousand shares of One pound (£1) each with the object
amongst others to finance an exploration party of prospec-

Page one of the agreement Lasseter signed before the CAGE expedition departed in July 1930. Despite Lasseter often claiming that he first stumbled on the reef in 1897, the document states that Lasseter found the gold reef in 1894, then returned there three years later with a 'surveyor'.

Blakeley recalled several occasions when Lasseter would do odd things before and during the expedition.

For starters, Lasseter slipped up when he was introduced to the highly regarded Alice Springs special magistrate and postmaster, Ernest Allchurch, shortly after they had arrived. According to Blakeley, Allchurch's knowledge of the Alice and its surrounds was exceptional; he had a razor-sharp mind, and had previously worked at the overland telegraph to Darwin.

Yet, as noted by Blakeley, Lasseter became quite chatty as he recalled the different buildings, including stables, harness shops and general storerooms, from his last visit there as a teenager:

'I came just after the great ruby rush was over and got supplies,' he said.

'That is a good bit over twenty-five years ago, mate,' replied Allchurch.

'Yes, I know that, I came here from Queensland to mine for rubies.'

'Well,' said Mr Allchurch, 'you don't remember those buildings for they are only a little over twenty years old.'[9]

But that didn't seem to deter Lasseter, who started talking about 'how he had come here and got fresh supplies'.

'From this station?' enquired Allchurch.

'Yes,' replied Lasseter.

'Well, old man, all I can say is that you dreamt it, for I have been station-master here for forty years and I am sure that never once did I issue stores to anyone. And I think if you stayed here I would remember you, because you must have been very young.'[10]

In *Hell's Airport*, Errol Coote recalled another telling visit to Allchurch, which he and Blakeley attended, 'with the conversation turning to Lasseter'.

> I asked him [Lasseter], said Allchurch, whether he called into the Post Office here when he passed through. He replied that he had camped to the north on the plains country, but had

> called in. He said there were only a few men here when he passed. Well, that is not the case. At that time there were nearly thirty men here. I think the exact number would be twenty-three. So, to my mind, he has never been here. The Post Office was about the only building here then, and, being an outpost, no man would make such a mistake about the number of men who would be here.[11]

There was no shortage of questions and doubts about Lasseter, both before and during the CAGE expedition. Blakeley noted in *Lasseter's Dream of Millions* how expedition member George Sutherland was particularly curious about how Lasseter had gotten to Cloncurry in Queensland all those years ago.

'In those days it was a pretty rough place,' said Sutherland.

'Oh,' Lasseter replied, 'I just had the mining fever, so I thought I would hop in the train and have a look at the new copper field.'

'You went out by train?' asked Sutherland.

'Yes, and a pretty rough trip it was too, but things were all excitement there over the new ruby find, so I thought I would go to the ruby fields.'

According to Blakeley, Sutherland let it be. However, he was well aware that Lasseter was talking about a time before the railway had come to Cloncurry. Sutherland would know, given he had worked on the construction of that railway line.[12]

And then there was the other condition that had been made on the agreement between Lasseter and CAGE before departing Sydney. This one required Lasseter to disclose any recognisable landmarks to the expedition party members once they were 50 miles from Alice Springs. With the arduous, sweat-inducing conditions and waning enthusiasm having set in, and being beyond this agreed radius, the expedition team was concerned that Lasseter hadn't yet seen something that would trigger his memory.

With the pressure mounting, suddenly he started remembering things, which, as Blakeley said, were more like oddities, rather than being anything of significance:

> There was a big fault in the granite rock about 600 feet up. Pointing to this he explained to us, 'See that cave up there — I can remember that I camped in there on my way out to the west.' I looked at him in astonishment, and to see if he was doing any leg pulling, but he seemed perfectly serious and I decided to hold my tongue. George grinned at me, and afterwards asked what I thought of the statement, since we both knew that nothing but an eagle had ever camped up there.[13]

It seems Lasseter was on a roll that day. 'That evening Lasseter went up to two bean trees, and patting them, said, "This is where I rigged up my hammock, between these two old cobbers [when he claimed to have passed through there before]."' But Blakeley was well aware that bean trees normally only live for about seventeen years at most, not thirty or more.[14]

Even the fact that Lasseter would sleep in the front cabin of the Thornycroft truck each night with the ammunition and rifle tucked under him seemed peculiar. Aside from feeling anxious about the possible attack of Aborigines, and not trusting any of the CAGE members, how did he cope when he was out in the desert by himself when he was younger?

As Blakeley recalled asking Lasseter, 'Why are you behaving like a new-chum that has never been out here before?'[15]

He also wondered why Lasseter had never made mention in any of his accounts about encountering any 'natives' when he first crossed Australia. Back then, it would have been impossible not to.

As has been recorded in various accounts, Lasseter's apparent lack of bush skills was also reflected in damper making, a staple for a bushman. When it came to his turn to make it, Blakeley indicated that he was clueless. Again, the expedition team wondered how Lasseter could have survived his desert crossing all those years ago. Mind you, it would have been a long time between visits, had he actually visited there in the first place.

On the other hand, there was a stage in the expedition when Lasseter indicated that the country would transform from being tough and almost insurmountable to splendid mineral-bearing country. To the expedition party's surprise, it did.

'It was one of the most extraordinary coincidences we encountered on this trip,' remembered Blakeley. 'As soon as Lasseter told me we were approaching where he thought the reef would be found, the character of the country changed completely.'[16]

With quartz and ironstone scattered throughout the area, things looked promising — until they got to Mount Marjorie. Besides being almost impossible to climb, when Lasseter took the reading with the sextant and then did his calculations from the summit, he declared the calculations were the same as in the bank vault in Sydney. This was also when he determined that they were 150 miles too far north. Instead, they had to head towards the Petermann Ranges, also known as 'breakaway country'. Even then, to head that much further south would increase the distance from Carnarvon significantly.

Add to that how back at camp that night Blakeley recalled Lasseter asking him if he remembered the bearings that he had taken that day. Apparently, he failed to write them down, yet originally indicated they matched those in the bank vault. Like so many things, it didn't make sense.

Furthermore, why did Lasseter leave it until 1929 before sharing his rich find publically?

Aside from my original theory of Lasseter forgetting where the reef was being incorrect, how did he know that it existed? He *must* have heard about it from someone else.

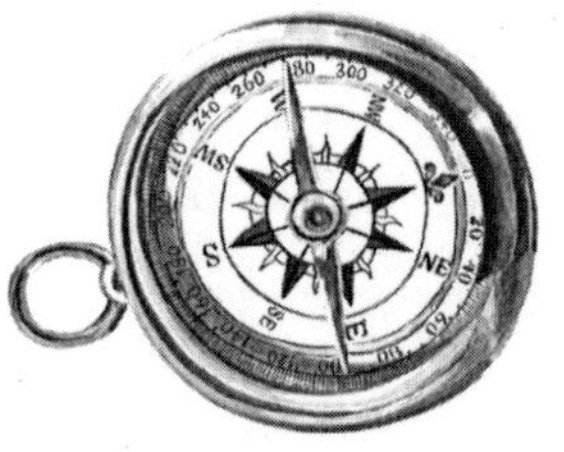

Chapter 8
Who was Harding?

I leaned back in my recliner chair and clasped my hands behind my head. As I gazed out the lounge room window across the front lawn, my brain ticked over recalling the various people that Lasseter claimed he'd encountered not long after he first stumbled on the quartz-bearing reef.

Then it hit me: Harding. This was a name that Lasseter consistently mentioned throughout his mind-boggling tale about attempting to relocate the reef, but did the mysterious man ever exist?

Oddly enough, in none of the accounts that I'd read about Harding was a first name, let alone a middle name or even an initial, ever used. They only referred to his surname. Did Lasseter simply pluck this surname, which was about as common as Smith back then, at random to make his story sound more plausible?

And what about his claims that Harding 'the surveyor' supposedly died while seeking financial backing for the gold reef? That seemed far too convenient.

Perhaps Lasseter, as Fred Blakeley suggested in *Lasseter's Dream of Millions*, borrowed the old tale about the skeleton of a dead man still clasping a bag of 'rich gold specimens' in the Western Australian desert, which was eventually found by a surveyor named Harding. According to Blakeley, 'Harding was of the opinion that this man could not have walked very far but in the course of a year or so the surveyor [along with a small team of miners] had found no traces of the reef.'[1]

A tenacious Harding then approached his good pal Sir John Forrest when he became Premier of Western Australia. He sent Harding out on a long, 'well-equipped camel expedition' to find the reef in Central Australia, but was unsuccessful, and later died with further attempts to locate it.[2]

There were so many theories circulating about Harding, but what struck me most was that they all focused on him being in the west and that his death was a common theme.

In view of me discovering the reef to the south-east of Alice Springs, I was determined to find out if Harding actually played a significant role in the knowledge of its existence. Again, it was all part of my attempt to disprove myself and, at the same time, prove that Lasseter hadn't discovered the reef in the first place.

Now given that the original consensus was that Harding was from Western Australia, and that he and Lasseter had travelled from Carnarvon to relocate the reef, this is probably how the misconception about the reef's actual location came about. In fact, all this line of thinking did was lead to hundreds of unsuccessful and often perilous expeditions, both personal and funded — including the use of the army and the media — to the west of Alice Springs.

Despite Bob Lasseter being inundated with enquiries about his father and the reef over the years, I made contact with him. I was aware that as part of threading Lasseter's story together, Bob, who was only six years old when his father died, had been looking into Harding as well. When I spoke with Bob on the phone, his calm yet resolute voice explained that his focus, like many others, had been on finding a Harding in Western Australia.

Although I was grateful for Bob taking the time to speak with me, when he said this, two thoughts occurred to me. One: was this due to Lasseter's well-worn yarn about Harding coming to his aid after he supposedly discovered the reef, then both men returning to relocate it? Or two: was it because a 'Harding's Reef' had purportedly been registered in Western Australia, with John Bailey claiming that he'd found documentation at the Department of Mines? Aside from geographic location, something was off. To me, these elements only added to the misbeliefs.

Remarkably, it wasn't long after my conversation with Bob that I realised that if someone was to obtain a Miner's Right in Central Australia, up and until 1911 they had to do this in South Australia, so I searched the State Records there. After sifting through an overwhelming number of references and files that contained the surname Harding, I found a Miner's Right that had been issued to a Joseph Harding in 1886. However, the document didn't state where Joseph Harding lived, nor where he had actually used the permit.

While staring at a map of Central Australia, I suddenly remembered that 1886 was when the so-called ruby rush, which surveyor and explorer David Lindsay instigated, had occurred near Arltunga. Furthermore, the ruby rush, or perhaps more appropriately the garnet rush, was well and truly over by 1897, when Lasseter, predominantly, claimed to have travelled there and then stumbled on his gold reef to the west of Alice Springs. By that stage, Arltunga was still in the throes of a gold rush, with it peaking in 1903 at the nearby Winnecke field, which ultimately became embroiled in Central Australia's first gold scam.

In order to determine if this was indeed the right Harding, let alone Joseph Harding, I needed to find out if he had spent time in or near Arltunga. Even more importantly, I needed to know that he had somehow come across the quartz-bearing reef that sits on the border of Queensland and the Northern Territory. Where to next?

In addition to exploring the State Records of South Australia, I went on a roadtrip with my son Daniel to the Australian Archives (now known as the National Archives of Australia) in Canberra. Among the plethora of old, faded documents I found a petition addressed to the 'Honourable Minister Controlling the Northern Territory'.[3] Dated 18 August 1899, the petition was created in view of Chinese migrants taking Australian miners' jobs. Since this was when

Arltunga was in its heyday, there's no doubt that prospectors would have come from far and wide, lured by the promise of striking it rich.

Tracing my finger down the document, at first I didn't notice anything. Then, as I studied the difficult-to-read cursive writing, this time from the bottom to the top, I was astonished to see that amid the various signed names of the residents of Arltunga was a 'contractor', Joseph Harding. My heart thumped loudly inside my chest. I was excited, curious and slightly nervous in the same breath. Was this *the* Joseph Harding I was looking for?

Despite both of the names Joseph and Harding being fairly commonplace, and being described as a contractor rather than a surveyor or prospector as Lasseter had previously mentioned, the petition reinforced that a Joseph Harding had worked and lived much closer to the gold reef that Michael and I had found.

Then, as I delved deeper into Joseph Harding, or Joe Harding or even Uncle Joe as he was often called by those men who roamed 'the north', I was amazed by how well-known and liked he was throughout the region back then. According to article interviews published in some former Adelaide newspapers, namely the *Mail* in 1924 and then the *Register* in 1925, he was a 'good-natured', hardworking and versatile man, who was sturdily built. Not surprisingly, some of the local Aboriginals would call him 'The Big Pfeller Boss'.[4] For an elusive man, he was rapidly coming to life.

But how did Joseph Harding come to be in Central Australia in the first place? From all accounts, he was born in Devonshire, England, then moved to Australia with his family when he was about two years old.

In young adulthood, with his brother Charles, he built a dock at Mannum, on the west bank of the lower Murray River, from where cargo-laden paddle steamers would chug through. By the time he was twenty, Harding progressively moved further north, working in places such as Blinman in the

Flinders Ranges (including the mine), Port Augusta and Port Pirie where he did wheat carting.[5]

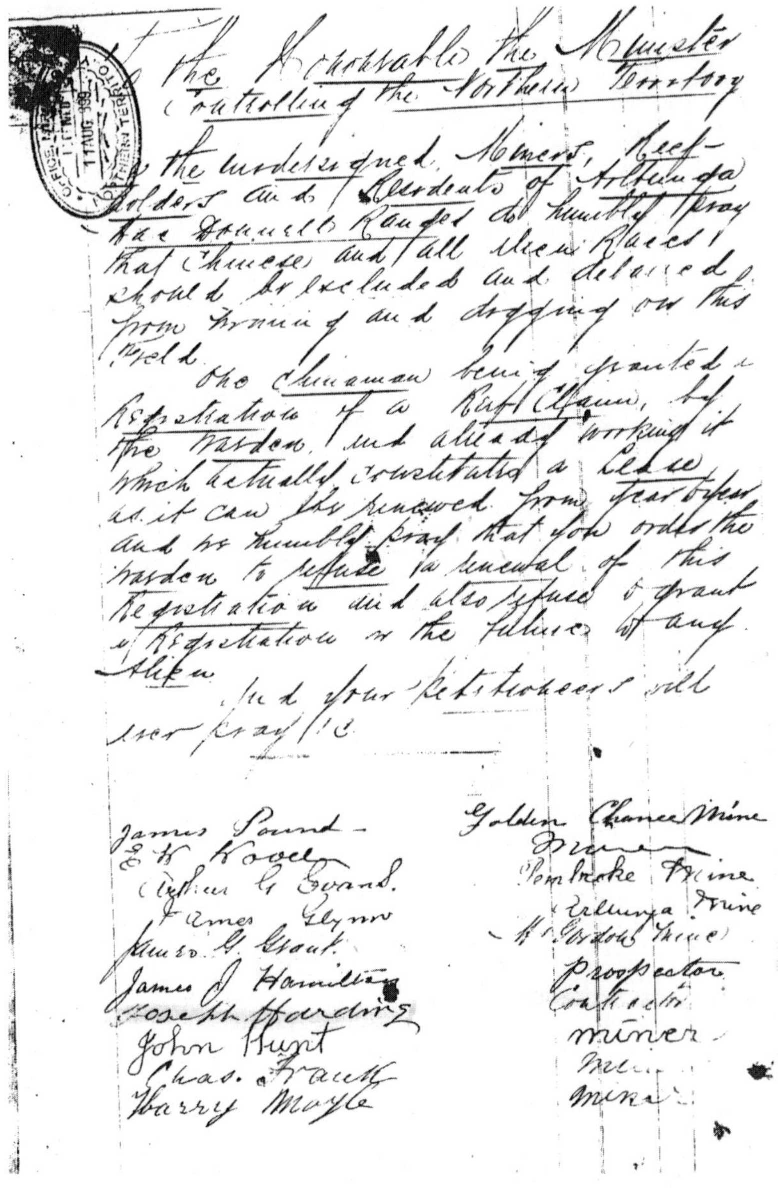

To the Honourable the Minister
Controlling the Northern Territory

We the undersigned Miners, Reef-holders and Residents of Arltunga and Donnell's Ranges do humbly pray that Chinese and all Alien Races should be excluded and debarred from Mining and digging on this Field.

One Chinaman being granted a Registration of a Reef Claim by the Warden, and already working it which actually constitutes a Lease as it can be renewed from year to year and we humbly pray that you order the Warden to refuse a renewal of this Registration and also refuse to grant a Registration in the future to any Alien

And your Petitioners will ever pray &c.

James Pound — Golden Chance Mine
E. H. Kool — Miner
Arthur G. Evans — Pembroke Mine
James Glynn — Arltunga Mine
James G. Grant — McGordon's Mine
James J Hamilton — Prospector
Joseph Harding — Contractor
John Hunt — miner
Chas. Franck — Mi[illegible]
Harry Moyle — miner

The petition addressed to the 'Honourable Minister controlling the Northern Territory', which includes contractor Joseph Harding's signature. His signature is fourth from the bottom on the left. (Australian Archives Series A1/1 Item 12/10343)

In 1872, he was contracted to carry government rations on bullock drays from Port Augusta to the stations along the Overland Telegraph Line to Alice Springs. After that, he was given another contract to work between the Alice and Barrow Creek.[6] Besides being gruelling work, based on the *Mail* article published on 12 April 1924, Harding was a hardy man who constantly had to adapt to survive the extremes of the arid interior:

> I was in the country when Dr Brown stocked Newcastle Waters ... I'll never forget that event. About the time that he went through we had 19 in. of rain in 14 days, and for five weeks my bullock teams and I were bogged. To cook our meals we had to build mud embankments and wade about up to our knees to attend to the fire when we got it going. For five weeks I slept; and practically lived on a bullock wagon. That happened in the Territory, and I have seen the other side of the picture. At Alice Springs the thermometer touched 124 degrees in the shade one summer. Even the crows died, and it takes a lot to kill a crow.[7]

There were other extraordinary hardships that he endured in Central Australia, especially in the early days. Water, as always, was the biggest issue in the dry backcountry, followed by lengthy periods of going without food. There were even times when he was almost penniless.

In the *Register* article, Harding recalls being desperately in need of water while travelling with his bullock team from Burt Creek to Tea Tree Wells, near the dried-out Woodforde River, north of Alice Springs:

> My bullocks had not tasted water for two days, and it looked like their finish. A half-wild black boy from a wandering tribe saved the situation. We asked him where we could find water. Putting his fingers to his lips, he said, 'Long time ago, Boss,

> water him sit down here.' I sank a well on the spot and struck a good flow at 9ft.[8]

According to Harding, the soak was named 'Harding's Well', given all soakage wells were named after those who discovered them.

During his roving years, I discovered that Harding was a 'government mail man' who delivered grog, clothing and parcels from Peake Station, near Oodnadatta in South Australia, to Alice Springs on horseback, with a team of pack horses carrying the mail. He also re-polled a section of the Overland Telegraph Line after the original wooden poles had rotted; drove horses from Alice Springs to Oodnadatta; and 'dealt in stock'.[9]

Despite the harsh and almost unbearable conditions, Central Australia was where Joseph Harding spent a significant part of his adulthood. For fifty-two years, he roamed the backcountry, a place where he seemed to belong.[10] He never lived in Western Australia. But I still needed to determine if and how he came to know about the quartz-bearing reef.

During the early stages of my research, one of the staff members from the Northern Territory Archives Service happened to call me and ask if I had read Richard "Dick" Kimber's book *Man from Arltunga*. It was the first that I'd heard of it, and I'm glad that she mentioned it. As it turned out, the biography, which tells the story of bushman and drover Walter Smith, who was born at Arltunga in 1893, was more illuminating than I ever anticipated. Most notably, I was stunned to read his vivid recollections about time spent with an affable and older Joe Harding.

As for Joe Harding, Smith recalled how he'd first moved to Central Australia in about the 1870s and eventually took on Crown Point Station, which was near the border of South Australia and the Northern Territory.[11] Apparently, Harding had already explored the wild and isolated country between

Birdsville in Queensland and the lower Finke River in the Northern Territory before settling at the property, where he had goats, cattle and horses.

Although not a formally qualified surveyor, I thought it interesting that Harding did some 'survey' work for the South Australian Railways in 1888. It was to do with the extension of the railway line from Oodnadatta to Alice Springs, which didn't officially commence until 1927. While Harding was learning 'the art of surveying' in the late nineteenth century, this is when it is thought that he became good friends with explorer David Lindsay. Harding also established the first pub at Arltunga — Paddy's Rockhole Pub in 1890, having been granted a licence by the Register of the Northern Licensing Bench in September of that year.[12]

However, I noticed in another document from the State Records of South Australia that Harding had signed a petition that opposed a publican's permit. No doubt this was done to thwart competition. The permit was approved by Winnecke and Arltunga Goldfields' Warden of the time, possibly to deter sly-grog selling, which Harding may have already been involved with.[13] According to the same document from the State Records, he was also the lessee of the Paddy's Hole well in 1894. In this instance, though, Harding was complaining about the rent. It seems he was both wily and enterprising.

Harding's other business interests included the Transcontinental Hotel at Oodnadatta, which was managed on his behalf when he owned it in 1905, and eventually Harding Springs Cattle Station, which now forms part of the Ambalindum pastoral station, located to the south of the Harts Range.[14]

Smith also mentioned in the *Man from Arltunga* that Joe Harding was in business partnership with the Arltunga butcher, Fred Klau, who happened to have a brother that worked in a butcher's shop in Cloncurry, Queensland.[15] No doubt the meat trade would have been booming. There would have been many exhausted prospectors to feed in the area.

As a young lad, Smith learnt some horsemanship from Harding, with Harding's methods described as both harsh and heartening. Smith then continued on with fellow horseman Billy "Colter" whose surname, according to author Richard Kimber, was formally known as Coulthard.

Harding's popularity in, and familiarity of, Central Australia was keenly noted by a visiting member of the South Australian Railway Commission, who'd wrote about Harding in 1887:

> It is not too much to say that Mr Harding is known to every inhabitant of the north, from Hergott (Marree) to Barrow's Creek. To him everything is fit and beautiful, and as we jog along he expatiates upon the virtues of bush, herb, or grass. Not a soul do we meet but he is accosted as an old friend, and not a horse is wanted that he will not lend.[16]

Despite Harding's jovial demeanour, various business interests, and constantly having to face the hardships of frontier life, my jaw just about dropped to the floor when Kimber describes Harding as having spent some time as a 'tea-and-sugar bushranger'.[17] From pinching the odd horse to stealing small mobs of cattle, more correctly known as cattle duffing, Harding, along with some mates, even pilfered eight hundred head of cattle from one of the properties owned by Australia's 'Cattle King', pastoralist Sidney Kidman. Harding's theory was to take just enough, but not too much, from those who had more than sufficient — and hopefully wouldn't notice.[18] How considerate of him.

Even in the transcribed 1903 diary of William Coulthard, the young nephew of Billy Coulthard, he recalls spending time mustering horses with an older Joe Harding. Besides a fit, youthful Coulthard having to ride with him on one occasion given Harding was 'to [sic] heavy to do any galloping', he also noted how another man by the name of Prosser came into their camp one night and accused Harding of stealing some horses.[19]

I was amazed that Harding never once got caught, especially with the stolen cattle. But, as Smith explained, Harding stuck to his surefire plan of moving the mob in the opposite direction to those that were normally moved south of the MacDonnell Ranges to Adelaide market. In Harding's case, he moved the cattle north and into the heart and less-traversed part of the Simpson Desert where, surprisingly, there was sufficient natural surface water.

> He [Harding] put couple of hundred at Harding Spring. And another place, a big waterhole called Pintjatjirrima back towards the Hale River, was used. He didn't leave too many there because the Arltunga police station was too close. He took them back to a place called Spriggs' old mine.[20]

The cattle were then taken to Dajarra and Camooweal, just over the border in south-west Queensland, as well as further north to Eva Downs and Newcastle Waters in the Northern Territory, where they were easily sold.

Pulling out a map, I retraced everywhere Harding had travelled with the cattle. I couldn't believe how close the cattle duffing route — towards the Queensland border — was to the giant quartz-bearing reef that Michael and I had found. Given that Harding would run the stolen cattle lower than yet still parallel to the original stock route to Queensland, this would have led Harding directly to the reef. No wonder he was never caught stealing cattle, because any searches by the constabulary only ever focused on the more accessible terrain and better-known trails in the south.

For me, all the landmarks, from the three hills that 'could not be mistaken' to the Quaker hat, fitted into place — exactly — especially since they could only be seen when going from west to east. It was yet another unforeseen element that supported my reference reversal theory.

There was something else, though, that Richard Kimber described in the *Man from Arltunga* that had me equally intrigued. So much so, I read it a few times. According to him, the Arrernte (pronounced Ah-runda) people, the traditional custodians of the land in and around Alice Springs, called the three breast-shaped hills near the quartz-bearing reef 'the breasts (teats) of the dingo'. Known as Urrinka-willartji, they formed part of the longer Dingo Dreaming route where a female dingo had given birth to her pups, and eventually returned there with them.

Then, Smith vividly recalled how another bushman by the name of Sandhill Bob told him the story about this fascinating yet understandably lesser-known Dingo Dreaming site:

> There was a big reef at Urrinka-willartji. Big as the sandhill. It was running south and east. And that is why them sandhills always get blocked by the outcrop and buried this old reef up then. It was a sort of a white rock. She had pups there then, and that's what that Dreaming is. That's where she had the pups.[21]

It has often been said by explorers, including metallurgist Des Stroud, who were focused on the south-western corner of the Northern Territory, that Lasseter's Reef was slowly covered in sand over the years. After reading this about the landscape of the Dingo Dreaming site, as well as having seen it for myself, it made perfect sense why this reef was not clearly seen in the south-east.

As for Harding, after living in Central Australia for almost fifty years, he sold all of his businesses and moved further down into South Australia, closer to Adelaide. Prior to that, Fred Klau had already taken over the Arltunga butcher shop, with him and his brother continuing to do business as usual — the stolen cattle were still being moved to Cloncurry.[22]

No wonder Harding, who was described as a 'jolly good fellow' at the beginning of the article published in the *Mail*, queried the writer with a chuckle, 'Now, who put you on to me? Darned if I think I can tell you much, but what I can tell you're welcome to.'[23] From all accounts, I'd think it would be more appropriate to describe Joseph Harding as a bit of a rogue, but a very likeable one. Then again, similar sentiments were expressed about Lasseter over the years, and, as I now realised, neither one of them was innocent when it came to the legendary gold reef.

Early days: crossing the Nullarbor for Perth, Western Australia, with my four-legged companion and a vague intention of finding Lasseter's Reef.

Motley crew: the Central Australian Gold Exploration (CAGE) Company members. From left to right: pilot Errol Coote, miner George Sutherland, driver Fred Colson, leader Fred Blakeley, mechanic Phil Taylor and guide Harold Lasseter at front. (National Library of Australia, Crome Collection)

The constant laying and relaying of coconut matting in the hot desert sand was tiresome but necessary to prevent the CAGE expedition vehicles from getting bogged. (Mitchell Library, State Library of NSW)

Despite being dubbed the best equipped expedition to the arid heart of Australia, the 1930 CAGE expedition was both backbreaking work and fraught with setbacks. (Mitchell Library, State Library of NSW)

The battered *Golden Quest* after Errol Coote's death-defying crash at Aiai Creek. (Mitchell Library, State Library of NSW)

German-born dingo scalper Paul Johns travelled with Lasseter and a string of camels to find the quartz-bearing reef. Johns was the last known European to see Lasseter alive. (Mitchell Library, State Library of NSW)

Errol Coote, a journalist and aviator, was engaged as the pilot of the *Golden Quest* and second-in-charge of the CAGE expedition in 1930. (Mitchell Library, State Library of NSW)

Shortly after replacing Fred Blakeley as CAGE's expedition leader, and while Lasseter was still missing in the desert, Errol Coote's decision to make camp at Ayers Rock (Uluru) backfired. (Mitchell Library, State Library of NSW)

Sydney's Daily Mirror *reports the discovery of Lasseter's body.*

SUPPLEMENT TO THE DAILY MIRROR

COMPOSITE NEWSPAPER

SYDNEY MIRROR

SAXA SALT Improves everything

IRON Jelloids Foundation of health

APRIL 29, 1931

OFFICIAL REPORT

LASSETER IS DEAD

Starvation ends his search for fabled gold reef

BODY IN SHALLOW GRAVE

ADELAIDE, Tuesday: Lewis Harold Bell Lasseter, the Sydney adventurer, explorer and prospector, is dead.

Lasseter died searching for the fabulously rich gold reef he claimed he once found. With his passing, the mystery of the location of the reef remains unsolved.

A report received from Alice Springs says that Lasseter's body was discovered in a shallow grave at Shaw Creek, at the ... of the Petermann Ranges ... covered with ...

... died of starvation while awaiting the delivery of rations, which his connections were to bring him.

Lasseter was last year appointed guide to an expedition into the Petermann Ranges in ... of the lost gold reef ... had been ...

Mr Lewis Lasseter . . . the mystery of a fabulous gold reef died with him.

Mr Robert Buck . . . his search for Lasseter ended at a shallow grave.

46

The front page of the *Sydney Mirror* on 29 April 1931 announces 'LASSETER IS DEAD'. Since then, hundreds of unfruitful expeditions have taken place to the west of Alice Springs. (Author's collection)

Central Australian cattleman Bob Buck led the search party in 1931 to find Lasseter. (Mitchell Library, State Library of NSW)

The restored Arltunga Gaol in the former gold rush town of Arltunga, Northern Territory, 1991.

Remains of an Arltunga miner's dwelling.

Leaving my two young children, Daniel and Alycia, behind while heading out on my maiden voyage to the Australian outback in 1991 was tough.

My two children from my first marriage, Catherine and Anthony, were strongly in my thoughts while in the desolateness of the outback.

Spotting the quartz blow for the first time in 1991. It led me straight to the other key landmarks surrounding the reef. Only later did I realise that the quartz blow was a landmark that Lasseter had mentioned in what became known as his diary.

Discovering the 'three hills' that Lasseter indicated 'could not be mistaken' to the east of Alice Springs was exhilarating.

The 'Three Sisters' with the tent-shaped hill on left.

An artistic impression of the 'three hills', or 'Three Sisters', with bell-shaped dresses on, not sun-bonnets as Lasseter described them. Seeing them as bell-shaped dresses is likely due to erosion occurring over the last hundred years or so. (Belinda Williams)

The tent-shaped hill.

The Quaker hat, as Lasseter described to Errol Coote all those years ago, has its 'top cut off' and can be seen in the distance.

Lee Shawsmith repairing a punctured tyre and the broken trailer spring that constantly gave us grief on the 1993 trip.

Heading in the right direction: the Land Rover and the trailer with the tent pitched on it, before heading out to the 'three hills'.

Left to right: Michael Valle, Lee Shawsmith and me in the Australian desert, with the tent-shaped hill in the background.

Me placing the Melton grassroots' syndicate members' names on Lasseter's Reef.

Spirited adventure: me and my trusty Land Rover spending a week at the reef.

Identifying the mountain range recorded in Lasseter's Diary, notably the page with MTL and MTE.

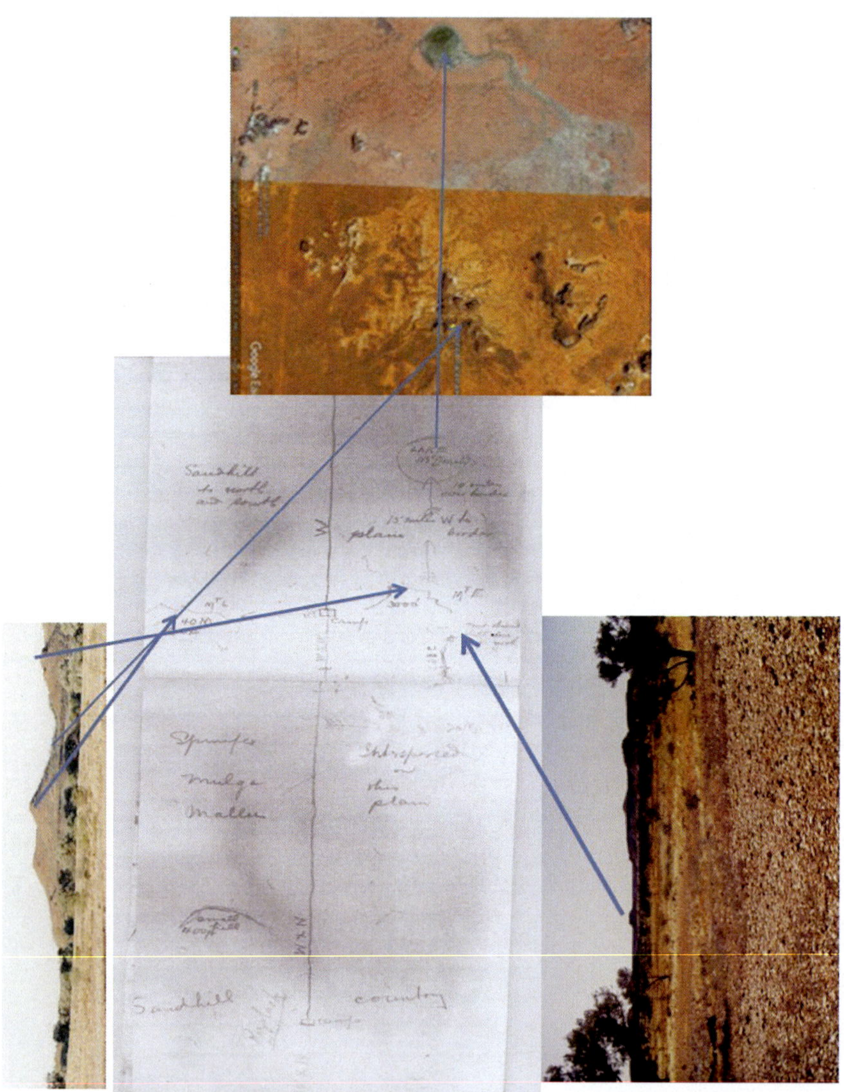

A remarkable likeness between my photos and the landmarks noted in Lasseter's Diary, all of which are located to the east of Alice Springs. (Lasseter's Diary image courtesy of Mitchell Library, State Library of NSW)

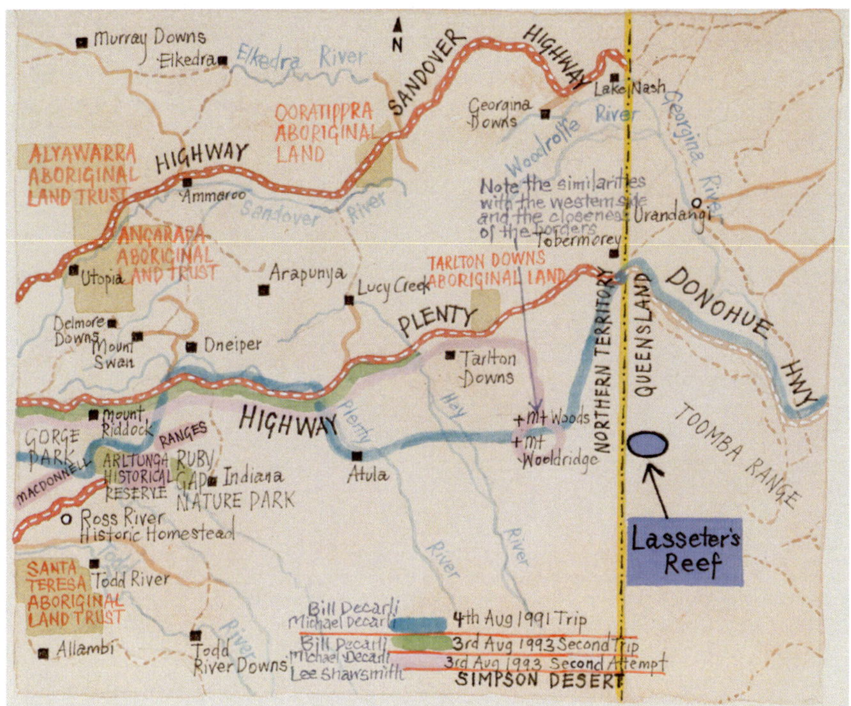

A map showing where my travel buddies and I ventured in 1991 and 1993 and discovered Lasseter's Reef near the Northern Territory and Queensland border. (Belinda Williams)

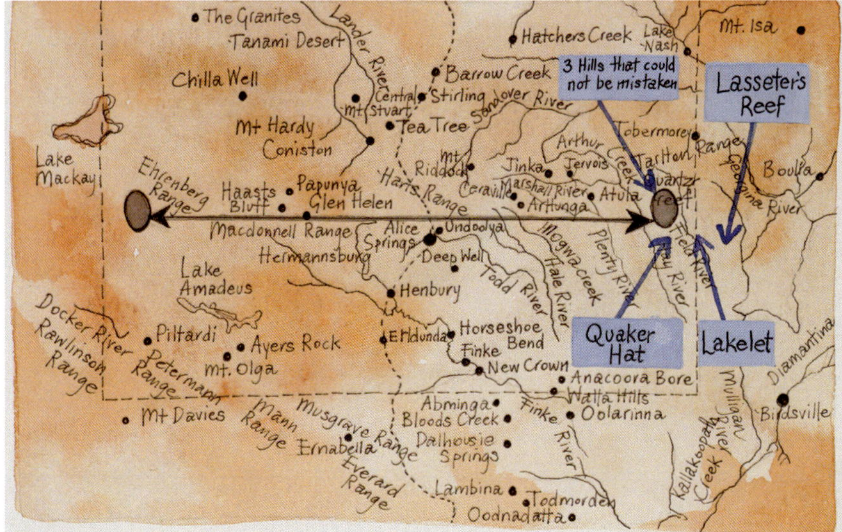

The real location of Lasseter's Reef as opposed to where Lasseter mistakenly believed it to be. To think that it all came down to a hunch after watching *The Legend of Lasseter* documentary in 1980. (Belinda Williams)

Artist impression of the top of a small section of Lasseter's Reef, based on a photo I had taken in 2019. (Belinda Williams)

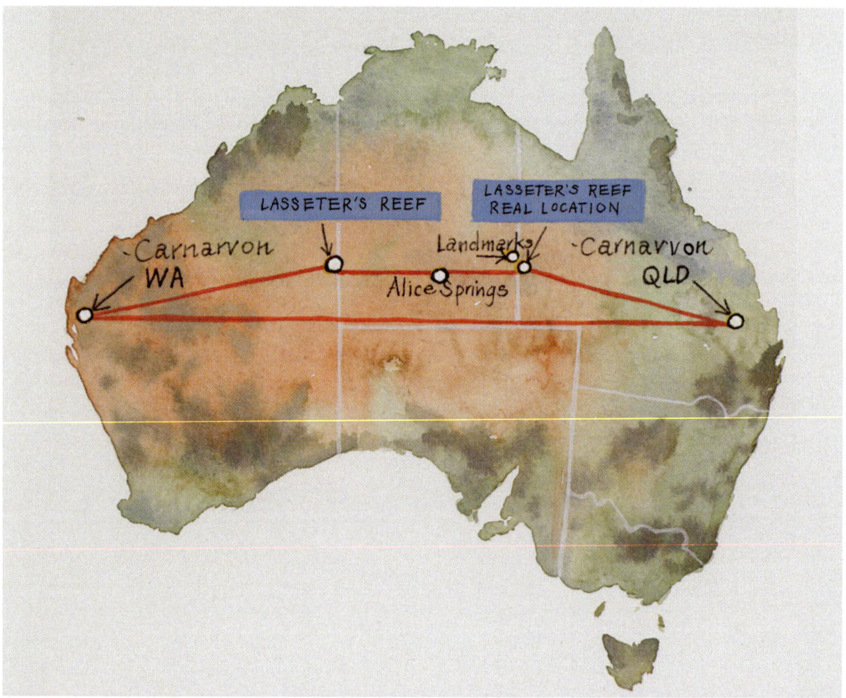

Carnarvon in Western Australia and the Carnarvon National Park in Queensland (simply referenced as Carnarvon here and which forms part of the Carnarvon Range) are virtually on the same latitude. (Belinda Williams).

My surface samples taken from the quartz-bearing reef are the same as what Lasseter described.

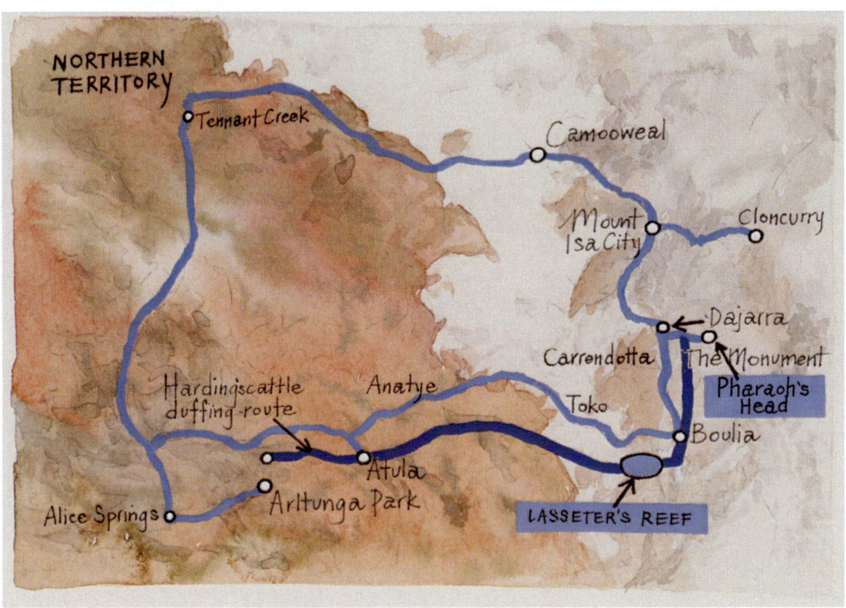

Joseph Harding's cattle duffing route clearly shows how close he was to all of the key areas and landmarks surrounding the gold-bearing reef. (Belinda Williams)

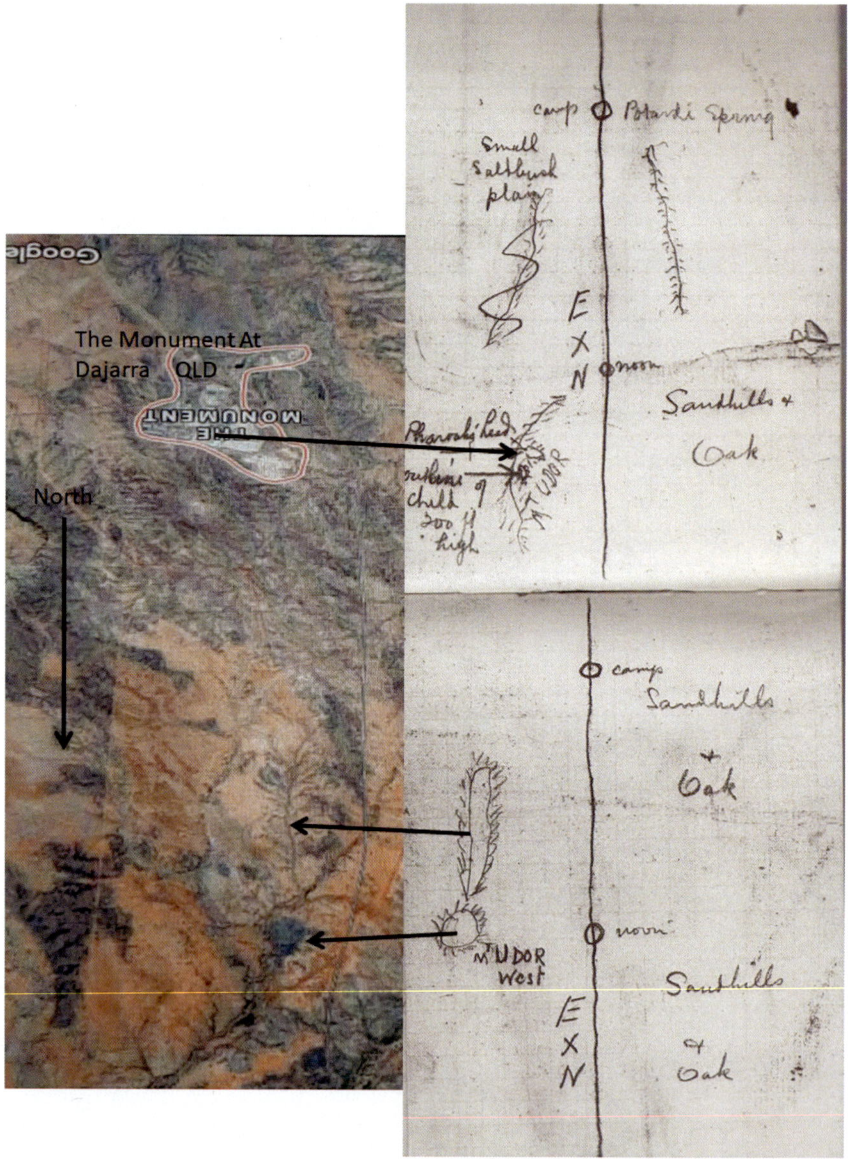

A modern day aerial image showing the location of Pharaoh's head (The Monument) near Dajarra, Queensland, and comparing that to the page where it is noted in Lasseter's Diary. There is a striking likeness to the topography where Mount Udor West and the lake immediately below it are noted in the diary.

Filming with American archaeologist, adventurer and TV host Josh Gates (standing centre) and the *Expedition Unknown* crew in the Northern Territory, 2016.

In threes: standing on Lasseter's Reef at the beginning of 2019. From left to right: Doug Wilson, me and Jason Faddoul.

After writing my first book about Lasseter's Reef in 2005, I was thrilled to learn that I was a grandfather. Kyle and Olivia are my eldest son Anthony's two children.

Me with my granddaughter Charli (on left) and daughter Catherine (on right).

Celebrating my forty-year journey with Lasseter's Reef and the best cheerleaders you could ever ask for. From left to right: me with my daughter Alycia, wife Pat and son Daniel.

Chapter 9
A Degree of Separation

Joseph Harding was one of several colourful, larger-than-life characters that Walter Smith had known in his long lifetime. Growing up in and living in the harsh, unforgiving country of the north, Smith, like many other men, took on various roles to survive. Not only was he an accomplished bushman, he was a widely travelled cameleer, gem fossicker, dingo trapper, fossil collector and prospector. From east to west and north to south, he would roam across the often burning-hot, thirsty terrain, taking him beyond the borders of the Northern Territory and over the shifting sands of the neighbouring states' deserts.

However, my mouth fell open when Smith indicated in the *Man from Arltunga* that he had a chance encounter with Lasseter before the CAGE expedition had set off from Alice Springs. In July 1930, Smith had returned from an unfruitful prospecting expedition (although he didn't find gold, he did find meteorite) with an Alice Springs local, Harry Hartley. When Lasseter met with Smith — who had been travelling with a string of camels — on one of his lone walks, he was interested in obtaining a couple of placid camels and additional supplies from him. The clandestine conversation then continued with Smith's mate, Frank Sprigg.[1]

According to Smith, Lasseter claimed to have already contracted German-born dingo skinner Paul Johns before departing the Alice. The deceptive twists were never-ending. In return for the docile camels and supplies, the ever-convincing Lasseter would provide Smith and Sprigg with a stake in his fabulously rich find. How could they decline, especially since Central Australia was in the grip of drought? Work was hard to come by.

Smith and Sprigg provided Lasseter with the necessary requirements, namely two camels, flour, a billy, and so on. Lasseter indicated that Johns wouldn't make an appearance until absolutely necessary, which he did, and would then split the expedition party so that Johns and Lasseter could continue the search to the south with the camels. As we know, Lasseter and Johns parted ways, and it was Smith's two docile camels that Lasseter continued travelling with and which subsequently spooked and bolted, disappearing into the desert scrub.

Later on, Smith and Sprigg became involved in the Eclipse Gold Expedition, which commenced from Oodnadatta.[2] As they moved through the Petermann Ranges, they found the deeply imprinted tracks of the camels that Smith had loaned to Lasseter. He too was convinced that Lasseter hadn't seen the reef, but had heard about it from someone else. However, was Smith aware that it had come from his old friend, Joe Harding? According to the *Man from Arltunga*, apparently not.

My main question now was, when and how did Lasseter and Harding actually meet?

In chapter 6, I mentioned how Lasseter had spent some time in Adelaide. He was there in 1917 doing various jobs and had re-enlisted in the army. He also had a head injury and was admitted to two different hospitals. By this stage, a senior-aged Harding was already living in or near Adelaide, having relocated from Central Australia a couple of years beforehand.

When I first looked for Joseph Harding's death certificate (before reading the articles published in the *Mail* and the *Register*) at the Births, Deaths and Marriages Registration Office in Adelaide, I found, among many, what I thought was the correct one. According to death certificate number 236, it stated that Harding was a farmer and his usual residence was Torrens Road in West Croydon, which is north-west of the

CBD, and not far from the Adelaide Hospital. Having died on 20 September 1922, aged eighty, the cause of Harding's death was nephritis, senility and cardiac failure. Given their respective health issues, I thought, at the time, that Harding and Lasseter may have met at the hospital as patients.

However, during the process of writing this book and with new information coming to light, a couple of things didn't fit. Firstly, the Joseph Harding from this death certificate was born in South Petherton in the Somerset Shire of England and came to Australia as an adult. When my daughter Alycia helped me look into this particular Joseph Harding's family background, and given the details in all of the other archival documents were consistent with the information that Walter Smith shared in the *Man from Arltunga*, I needed to do another search. Sure enough, there was another Joseph Harding.

Based on death certificate number 496 from the Births, Deaths and Marriages Registration Office in Adelaide, Joseph Harding was a grazier who'd moved from England at two years

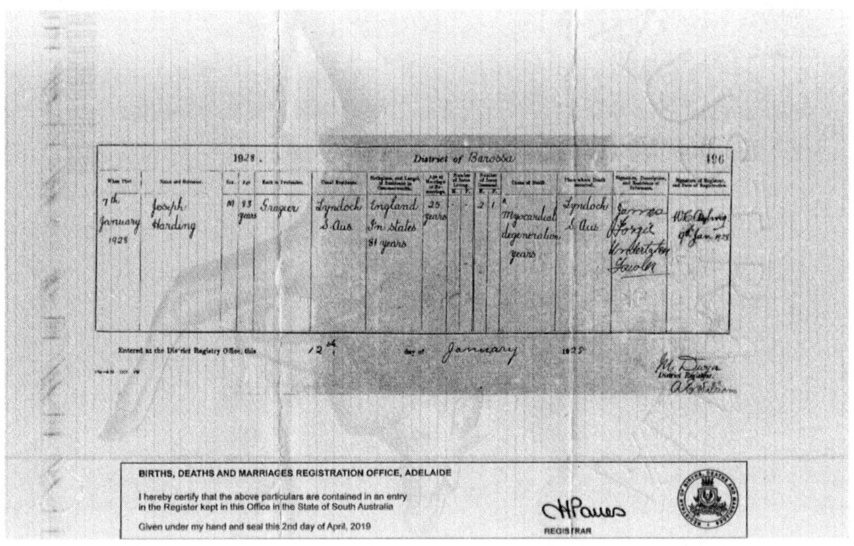

1928. District of Barossa 496

7th January 1928 | Joseph Harding | M | 93 years | Grazier | Lyndoch S. Aus | England In states 81 years | 25 years | 2 1 | Myocardial degeneration years | Lyndoch S. Aus

Entered at the District Registry Office, this 12th day of January 1928

BIRTHS, DEATHS AND MARRIAGES REGISTRATION OFFICE, ADELAIDE

I hereby certify that the above particulars are contained in an entry in the Register kept in this Office in the State of South Australia

Given under my hand and seal this 2nd day of April, 2019

REGISTRAR

Death certificate no. 496 for Joseph Harding, showing that he died of myocardial degeneration on 7 January 1928. (Births, Deaths and Marriages Registration Office, Adelaide)

of age. On 7 January 1928, he died at the age of eighty-three from myocardial degeneration. His permanent address, up until then, was listed as Lyndoch, a town near Gawler in the Barossa Valley, which is about 56 kilometres from Adelaide. The death notice in the *Chronicle*, dated 14 January 1928, also confirmed many of these details.[3]

However, in the *Register* newspaper article dated 29 August 1925, it said that Joseph Harding had been living with his niece and nephew, Mrs and Mr EJ Dennis of 26 West Street, Torrensville.[4] And according to the article published in the *Mail* the year before, Joseph Harding, or 'Uncle Joe', was just as popular in the suburbs of Adelaide as he had been in the north.

When I looked at a map of Adelaide, Torrensville is only a short distance to the west of the CBD, while Lasseter's sister, Lillian McGrath, lived at College Park, which is just north of the city. I was gobsmacked: these two addresses were even closer. Alternatively, Lasseter, as we know, had noted his 'permanent' address as Port Adelaide, which is further north of Torrensville. Either way, my theory was correct: both Lasseter and Harding were in Adelaide in 1917.

As to how Harding and Lasseter met is anyone's guess. It could have been that they connected at a nearby park, a pub or an event. Based on their residential addresses at the time it is possible that they were even on the same bus route, especially if Lasseter was coming from Port Adelaide into the city proper. Perhaps they met while Harding was on his way to or attending a doctor's appointment.

The reason I say this is because the *Mail* article published in 1924 reported that Joseph Harding weighed 19 stone — the equivalent to a hefty 121 kilos — and included a photograph that portrayed him as portly and ruddy faced.[5] (Despite his stern look in the black and white photograph, I still detected a steely glint in his eye.) And, as indicated on his death certificate, he died from myocardial degeneration. Meanwhile, one of the other Adelaide newspaper articles stated that he had 'slightly impaired hearing' in his senior years.

No matter how Lasseter and Harding met, from all accounts both of these men were quite engaging, colourful and talkative. Having read all of the information about Harding's life, I started to notice the parallels with how Lasseter had created his own version of the story. He had used Harding's words. For instance, Harding was not a surveyor, or even a government surveyor, but had learnt the 'art of surveying' when the railway was being considered in the late 1800s.

However, Harding was contracted by the government to deliver the mail — and solo on horseback. Lasseter had also mentioned key locations such as how he'd travelled from Cloncurry in Queensland via the ruby fields near Arltunga to Alice Springs in the Northern Territory, all places that Harding had roamed. Lasseter also claimed twice that

JOSEPH HARDING, "THE LAST OF THE OLD-TIMERS."

'The Last of the Old-Timers': rugged bushman Joseph Harding, fondly called 'Uncle Joe' by Torrensville residents while he was living there, appeared in an article in *The Mail*, 12 April 1924, Adelaide. (National Library of Australia)

he'd travelled from Oodnadatta to relocate the reef, even mentioning the hotel there. Again, it was a place that Harding had been to, and, at one stage, owned the pub.

Lasseter also talked about how thirsty the land was, given the shortage of water, something else Harding spoke of. Then, of course, Lasseter described the landmarks surrounding the reef exactly as Michael and I had found them in the east. Most of all, it is exactly where Harding had been cattle duffing all those years ago. No wonder Harding didn't want anyone to originally know about his find or make a claim: he was too popular in the backcountry. Instead of striking it rich, he would have ended up in a gaol cell for his 'tea-and-sugar bushranging'.

Or perhaps, given how isolated the area surrounding the reef is, securing finance and getting a sufficient water supply there back then was going to require a phenomenal amount of funding and manpower. Having seen what Arltunga went through, and based on his personal experiences, I started to wonder if Harding understood that water was worth more than gold.

But why did Harding tell Lasseter about the reef? Was it because he knew that he wouldn't get out there again at that late stage of his life? Or did he think a confident middle-aged Lasseter could spruik it before his time was up?

Besides, had Harding given Lasseter the gold nuggets to prove that it existed? And when Harding shared the details about the reef, did he say it was to the east or west? Was he testing Lasseter's mettle by using the old prospector's trick and army technique of reversing the bearings and/or landmarks? Or had Lasseter simply gotten confused with place names, such as Carnarvon, and the location of the landmarks, given he'd never been there in the first place?

With Joseph Harding dying in 1928, it was one year later that Lasseter decided to go public with his knowledge of his fabulously rich find. Did Lasseter deliberately hold off to claim the gold-bearing quartz reef for himself? He was in a dire financial situation. Or did he do it to protect Joseph Harding?

One thing we do know is that Lasseter didn't start sharing any knowledge of the reef with his family until after 1917. Then, as of 1929, after he officially approached Albert E. "Texas" Green, he would start mentioning the name Harding. Did Lasseter want to honour the role that Joseph Harding had played? Or did John Bailey, the president of the AWU and director of CAGE, who had a chequered past, advise Lasseter that the story about the reef was more believable if he said he'd found it, not Harding? And whenever Harding's name was mentioned, was it suggested that Lasseter only refer to him by his surname? I believe that having Lasseter say he was the man who originally found the reef was done purely to secure financial backing for the CAGE expedition. Sadly, it all came down to greed.

Even with all of my searches, I never came across the document that Bailey claimed to have found about a Harding's Reef being registered in Western Australia, or any record of it at the Department of Mines. Then again, it is thought that several of the CAGE documents were destroyed, although it is hardly surprising — the entire set-up was rife with skulduggery.

As to why Lasseter noted in his diary that he located and pegged the reef — despite not actually doing so — before dying in the desert, I believe that since he was starving, had sandy blight and was most likely hallucinating, it was his way of acknowledging that he knew that the reef existed.

I can understand why there was so much confusion about the reef's location, but there's no doubt that Joseph Harding was the key to the reef's existence and ultimately Lasseter's knowledge about it. Because if my theory was wrong, why did I find a gold-bearing quartz reef approximately 300 miles (482 kilometres) to the east of Alice Springs based on the *exact* same landmarks Lasseter had described to Errol Coote during the CAGE expedition, and where Harding had roamed with stolen cattle for all those years?

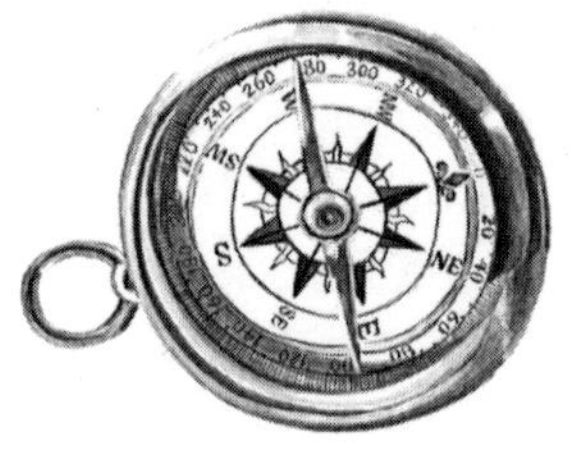

CHAPTER 10

RETURNING TO THE REEF

At the beginning of 1993, the little bell over the delicatessen door rang as the local bank manager strode in. He'd come to place his customary order. While slicing some meat and cheese for him, he looked around the shop in slow motion and asked me about the photo display. Pointing to the photo of the three hills, I explained to him how I'd found Lasseter's Reef, and how it was discovered by Joseph Harding in the first instance. The bank manager's eyebrows shot up.

'I'd always thought that the whole concept of Lasseter's gold reef was a hoax,' he said.

As he continued to listen to me and take a good, long look at each of the photos, his uncertainty had changed to enthusiastically nodding his head in agreement: he believed that the reef did in fact exist.

An even greater surprise, though, was when he said, 'Why don't we start a syndicate?'

By February, a meeting was held for those interested in being a part of it. It was thought best that there be a maximum of nine members from the community. And just like that, a grassroots syndicate was formed and some money was raised to fund another expedition. It was decided that the next trip to the reef take place towards the latter part of winter that year. It would be a little less than six months before I was back in the desert.

In the lead up to departing on 3 August 1993, I designed a new and improved off-road camper trailer that, I thought, would better withstand the harsh and ever-changing desert terrain. It was then meticulously built by Russell Rundle, who was one of the syndicate members. My nephew Michael was keen to rejoin me on the second trip. This time, however, there would be three of us going out to the reef. Michael's mate, Lee Shawsmith, a fellow band member who pounced on the opportunity to join the syndicate, was going to come with us.

After a high-spirited going away party, and many more people than the first trip to bid us goodbye, Michael, Lee and I departed for the gold reef in the heart of the Australian outback. Given Michael and I had encountered some significant delays and obstacles on the first trip, especially with that nightmarish effort of crossing the Hay River, we'd already planned to cross it closer to the Plenty Highway. I knew exactly when we would hit the right spot: I'd carved Pat's and my initials in a tree on the first trip. From there, we could pick up the same track we used last time to make our way to the reef.

Overall, the journey to Alice Springs went well, barring the Land Rover's headlight fuses blowing out at dusk. Then about an hour later, we came across a mob of cattle lingering on the road not far, and somewhat ironically, from the intersection of the Lasseter and Stuart highways. Despite driving at a crawling pace in what had become pitch darkness and veering left then right to avoid them, a cow was hit. The damage to the vehicle was minor in comparison to the bloody, gut-wrenching mess on the side of the road.

After staying overnight at the truck stop at Alice Springs, we headed out on the Plenty Highway for the desolate interior, and what was to become a much rougher journey than anticipated. Turning onto a track about 80 kilometres past Jervois Station, the purpose-built trailer started rattling around, threatening to fall apart. The trailer springs couldn't bend while the D-shackles were a couple of inches too short. Then there were the flat tyres, which amounted to more than twenty for the entire trip.

We'd barely started and we were already without spare tyres for the trailer. Although Lee suggested that we temporarily leave the trailer behind, I explained to him that if we did that, we'd never find it again. Besides having the trailer tent, we needed every drop of water and fuel that we could take, and the Land Rover was already packed to the brim with food and equipment. Determined, we continued to the Hay River crossing, but the trailer springs couldn't cope, constantly requiring us to stop, check and readjust them.

Tired and frustrated, we set up camp later that day. I did what I could to reinforce the springs with chains and tyres by torch and in the dim glow of firelight. Meanwhile, Michael played some rhythmic beats on a drum pad and Lee twanged his guitar. Besides needing to continue practising their instruments, they helped keep our spirits up.

Next morning, as I was the first to get up, I made a breakfast of fried eggs and beans. Afterwards, I wandered over to a small, nearby mountain to get my bearings. When I clambered to the top of the short, steep hill, no matter which direction I looked, I couldn't see the vehicle. I'd temporarily misplaced myself.

Descending down from the hill, I decided to time myself and eventually found my way back to camp within about twenty minutes. Blissfully unaware of where I'd been, Michael and Lee were finishing off their breakfast when I arrived. Straight away, I encouraged them to take a two-way radio and go up the same mountain I had. I asked them to radio me when they were on their way back.

Sure enough, they climbed up the mountain and not really seeing anything majorly interesting, and wondering why I'd sent them there in the first place, they radioed me when they were returning. I expected them to arrive back at camp in twenty minutes. They didn't. There was no sight of them.

After that, I climbed on top of the Land Rover and started to call them on the radio. They had missed the vehicle by 100 metres and were walking straight into the arid heart — the desert. My intention was to show them how easy it was to get lost out there, but I didn't think they would go quite that far off course.

With their heads hanging low in embarrassment, they returned. Later on, Lee came to me and admitted, 'I now understand why you said we couldn't ditch the trailer before.' He then went to grab his diary, indicating that he wanted to tell me something. Reading aloud a line he'd written the night beforehand, he said, 'I think the desert is affecting Bill's judgement.' Then he quickly added, 'I'm so sorry, Bill.'

After that, we packed up camp. As we continued to the east to follow the line of the sand dunes to the three hills, the springs snapped. Not being able to continue over the increasingly bumpy terrain, I put an old tyre between the springs and the trailer, then headed north and followed one of the property tracks at Marqua Station, a cattle station located near the Queensland border. However, it wasn't the most cordial welcome when we arrived there.

Three four-wheel drives loaded with guns appeared from the corrugated trail, with thick red dust trailing behind them. As they jumped out of their vehicles, with stern faces and hands on hips, the station manager at the time, Connor Coombe, and his station hands accused us of having cut down some of the property's fences. But that wasn't the case.

'As a matter of fact,' I started to explain, 'your fence was already down and all we did was put it back up and knock it back in again.'

Tilting the wide brims of their hats, the tone of the conversation promptly turned from defensive to respectful and accommodating.

I then told Connor why and where we'd driven from deep in the desert, and how our trailer springs had completely busted. Slowly shaking his head in disbelief, he was flabbergasted by the trip we'd just done. He jokingly started calling us 'the desert rats'. After giving each one of us a firm handshake and a hearty slap on our backs, Connor invited us to stay overnight at the Marqua campsite, near the homestead. We gratefully accepted.

The following day, I repaired one of the tyres with gaffer tape and a liquid patch puncture sealant. Connor kindly helped us with the trailer. He even gave us a spring and another tyre to ensure that we got back to Alice Springs via the Plenty Highway. Some significant repairs and new parts would be needed before we could head back out into the gruelling desert, and that was going to require more time and money.

I rang Pat to let her know what happened to the trailer and the tyres and asked her to contact the syndicate members to see how they felt about the situation. When we spoke again, she said, 'Everyone's happy for you to do whatever's necessary to get out to the reef.'

After camping for the best part of a week at the back of the Alice Springs truck stop, the repairs to the trailer were almost done. Even the sudden torrential downpour of rain, which saw a leaking tent, soaking wet clothes and becoming more like bedraggled rats than desert rats, didn't deter us.

Once everything was sorted, dried — partly with a clothes drier in the toilets — and packed, we headed straight back to the homestead at Marqua Station via the highway. The idea was that we would follow the track from there to the eastern side of the Hay River, then head south and follow it until we found our original crossing. From there, we would travel directly to the landmarks surrounding the reef. Unlike the two long and arduous weeks it took Michael and me to traverse the desert and river on the 1991 trip to get to the quartz-bearing reef, coming from this direction, remarkably, only took us a day to get exactly where we needed.

Before reacquainting ourselves with the three round hills and the reef, we met with Connor again at Marqua Station, advising him of our intentions. This time we brought him a box of fresh fruit. His face lit up when he saw it. It is a real treat for those who live in the outback. They don't get it very often.

With Connor's all clear, it wasn't long before we were slowly rising up and descending from steep sand dunes, in between carefully navigating our way through the dense pockets of mulga. On the top of a tall sand dune I stopped the Land Rover, jumped out and took a bearing with the compass. There they were, as clear as clear can be: the three hills that 'could not be mistaken', the Quaker hat in the distance and the reef with its giant quartz blow. Although there are a few Quaker hats in this area, when looking at this particular one in relation to the reef and the three hills, these distinctive landmarks are in triangulation.

My heart swelled with excitement, just like it did the first time Michael and I came here, and my smile broadened with each inhale. I rushed back to the car, enthusiastically calling out to Michael and Lee, wondering why they hadn't gotten out yet. As I got to the car door, they were stretching and yawning. They'd just woken up. All that jostling around while I was driving towards the reef must have rocked them to sleep.

As it was Lee's first time out there, he exclaimed, 'We can't be here already!' He couldn't believe that we'd hit upon the reef so quickly, particularly since we'd approached it from a different direction.

This time, we were camping on the bare and expansive red claypan, between the three hills and a waterhole, and making our way around the reef entirely on foot for a week. The idea was that becoming familiar with the landmarks surrounding the reef would minimise the risk of getting lost, as did keeping the trailer in one place with the tent pitched on top of it. In the desert, you always have to keep your wits about you.

After setting up camp, we got the fire going. While it crackled and popped, we boiled the billy. Before bed, I facetiously said to Michael, 'It's okay to sleepwalk in your own tent tonight, mate.' Right from the outset of this trip, the three of us had an agreement about our sleeping arrangements. Whoever was the last to go to bed at night would have to sleep in the middle of the three-person tent. However, earlier on in the week, when we'd camped near the Plenty Highway, it was Michael's turn to sleep in the middle. We were all asleep, until there was an almighty scream. Michael, still asleep, scrambled towards the closed tent opening. Straight away I lurched forward to grab hold of him. If he kept going, the entire tent and the three of us would have crashed heavily down on the ground.

It was only when I lightly teased Michael about it that he shared his frightening dream. 'I felt like I was floating above my body,' he recalled, 'and when I looked down, it wasn't just me that I saw sleeping, I saw you and Lee as well. That's when I screamed.'

As the cattle hadn't travelled down that far, the tall green grass surrounding the claypan and the reef waved gently in the breeze. When we had a wash each the morning, chatty finches would flit and flocks of green and gold bush budgies would fly all around us. When we threw the water away, butterflies with their distinguished black, white and yellow markings would silently flutter above, then land on it for puddling.

It was while I was having a wash one morning that I noticed how the area was suitable for keeping cattle safe and content with sufficient grass and permanent water, while the surrounding hills and rocky outcrops acted like natural boundaries or holding pens. I could only imagine how Joseph Harding and his men would stop there to graze, fatten and hide the mobs of cattle they'd stolen.

With each passing day, we collected more and more sharped-edged rock samples as we combed different parts of the reef, took photos and became at one with the landscape. The finale was hammering the board with the datum references, along with all of the syndicate members' names and addresses, onto the reef itself. On the one hand, Michael, Lee and I had achieved what we'd set out to do. On the other hand, something was bugging me.

I recounted in my mind, like a checklist, all of the things we'd done. It wasn't until the next day, as I crawled out of the tent, that I realised what *it* was. There in front of me, about 500 metres in fact, was what I believe to be the mountain Lasseter had sketched an outline of in his diary, based on what Joseph Harding had originally told him. Or perhaps Harding had drawn it for Lasseter in the first place.

Either way, the page that I am referring to had MTL on it, which was to the left of the campsite in the diary, therefore was logically referring to a mountain on the left or in a south-easterly direction, despite some potentially thinking it was an abbreviated form of Mount Leisler (also known as Mount Marjorie). Then, to the right of the camp, on the same page, was a large mountain referred to as MTE.[1] However, I'm uncertain what that actually refers to. Based on the directions used on those diary pages, it isn't Mount East.

Just below that, though, is a scrawling that says 'tent shaped hill due north', followed by MTR, which most likely meant mountain to the right. The mountain I was looking at, which, despite subsequent searches, appears to be nameless, was yet another landmark to substantiate that the reef existed to the east of Alice Springs. Although it had taken me until the last day of camping there to actually spot it, it was the beginning of being able to put some of the drawings from Lasseter's Diary on the ground.

Grabbing the camera, I noticed that there was only one picture left on the frame counter. I'd used up all of the film. We'd been so busy documenting and scrutinising every detail over the past week. With that final photo of the mountain taken, it was time to head back to Melbourne, but not without difficulties.

As we were coming out of Marqua Station, I drove over a steep and craggy hill and suddenly heard an ear-piercing scraping sound. 'What's that?' the three of us exclaimed in unison, while wincing.

With the engine still running, I got out to check all around and beneath the trailer: the rear axle was twisted. Despite this, we slowly made our way back to the Plenty Highway by nightfall. We were now low on fuel. Whether it was sheer determination or something else looking out for us, we got within a few kilometres of the Atitjere Store in the Harts Range. The store was closed but we decided to camp nearby for the night.

With a fiery red sunrise appearing the next morning, it was only a couple of hours later that the Aboriginal-run store was open and we were able to refuel. I called Pat from the payphone to let her know that we had everything we needed and that we were making our way back to Melbourne.

After finishing our call, I glanced at the trailer in the carpark: the trailer hooks had been stripped bare. Fortunately, a kind local Aboriginal man was able to weld them back together, but once we got back on the highway, the damaged axle continued to give us grief. With the trailer wheels being out of alignment, they would constantly blow out. To avoid any further delays, or ditching the trailer, we stopped to do our own wheel alignment, using what spare tyres were left, then bought two new ones. From then on, the journey home was fairly straightforward.

Chapter 11

Down to a Bearing

I couldn't contain my excitement any longer. I was dying to share my story about Lasseter's Reef with the world. But shortly after arriving back in Melton, a meeting with the syndicate members was arranged and everyone bar myself decided it would be best to keep it to ourselves — for the time being. There were still some steps that we needed to take, including applying to the Northern Territory's Department of Mines, given we required an exploration licence for the area surrounding the Hay River. I had to wait.

In the meantime, I arranged for the jagged quartz samples that Michael, Lee and I had taken from the surface of the reef to be analysed. While that was taking place, another significant element that would reinforce that Lasseter's Reef was to the east, not the west, came to my attention.

When Lee, Michael and I drove through Alice Springs, I picked up a Shell road map of Australia from one of the service stations. On the back of it, it had a lot of the gemstones that could be found throughout the country. I thought it would be handy for identifying things whenever we were out gathering rock samples. It wasn't until I was tidying up at home that I turned it back over to the side with the map on it and placed my right index finger roughly where the reef is located on the border. Then I looked across to see that there was a Carnarvon National Park in central Queensland — and it was virtually on the same latitude as Carnarvon in Western Australia!

Again, I was completely taken aback. Was this how Lasseter got the location muddled? Did Harding say

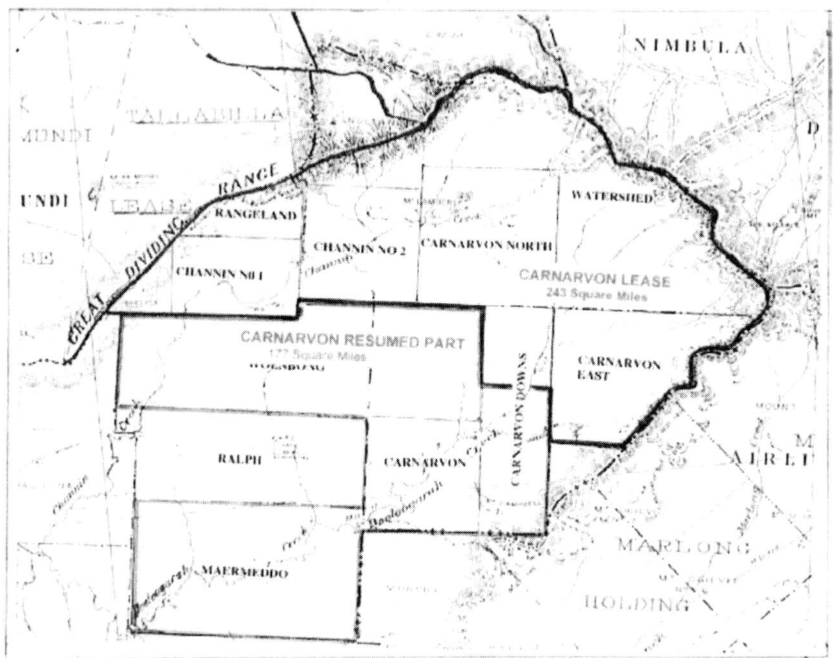

A map showing the 1889 leaseholds and resumed parts of what was known as Carnarvon, Queensland. (Courtesy of Queensland Police Museum)

Carnarvon to him, forgetting that there was another in Western Australia? Or was it simply because people who live in outback regions, like Harding did, usually call places by the first part of their name only, not the full name such as Carnarvon Gorge, Carnarvon Range or Carnarvon Station (now a reserve), all of which are located in or near that region. Even then, I did come across some old maps dating back to about 1900 which only had Carnarvon printed on them for this central region of Queensland.

I also discovered that to the east of the gorge was a sizeable reserve called Carnarvon, which was renamed Rewan in 1909 when it became the Queensland Police Horse Breeding Station.[1]

Best of all, and according to Google Earth nowadays, the reef is approximately 275 miles (443 kilometres) east of Alice Springs and approximately 650 miles (1046 kilometres) west from the centre of Carnarvon National Park. Despite the variations and/or discrepancies in various literature about the distance to the infamous gold-bearing reef from Alice Springs and Carnarvon in the past, these Google Earth readings are pretty much within the range of what has been recorded historically: about 700 miles (1126 kilometres) from Carnarvon and 300 miles (482 kilometres) from Alice Springs.

Mind you, the techniques used to calculate distances back then were a bit different to what's currently available. And then, of course, there were those who were constantly changing the distance to make it fit in with Carnarvon in Western Australia. Nonetheless, these distances fitted with the distinguishing landmarks that I'd discovered in the east.

Furthermore, this is exactly how the border of the Northern Territory and Queensland acts like a mirror image to the distances to the border of Northern Territory and Western Australia. Although the latitude is the same (there's less than half a degree of difference) as what Lasseter indicated with the coordinates left in the Bank of Australasia before the CAGE expedition commenced, not surprisingly the longitude didn't match, because he didn't know where it was in the first place.

The other thing that I discovered about the Carnarvon region in central Queensland is that given it became known as a permanent site of water, it was ideal for grazing sheep (initially), cattle and horses. In the 1860s, Carnarvon Station was established, consisting of a number of blocks or runs. Meanwhile, cattle drives were known to take place through nearby Carnarvon Gorge. It also seems, according to a chronicle of Carnarvon, that cattle duffing and horse stealing were rife at Carnarvon Station in the late 1890s, which was mostly attributed to infamous brothers and bushrangers Patrick and James Kenniff.[2] Then, from about 1898 until 1903, the region, like most parts of northern and central Australia, was in severe drought. However, people were known to come from all over to graze and save their valuable stock at the still grass-covered Carnarvon Station.

But how did Joseph Harding know about Carnarvon in central Queensland? Did he simply use it as a reference point to determine distances, especially since it was on a similar latitude to Alice Springs? Or did his cattle duffing mates form some kind of tag team, whereby they drove stolen cattle west of Carnarvon Station to onsell at Cloncurry and Dajarra?

It suddenly occurred to me that when Lasseter had placed the bearings for the location of the reef inside the envelope and put it in the Bank of Australasia, the real compass bearing had been right there all along.

At the bottom of the front of the envelope, Lasseter had written that a bearing of '274°E at Carnarvon' had been taken with a compass. Lasseter had the exact location without even realising it, but he mistakenly assumed that the bearing was to be used east of Carnarvon in Western Australia.

When looking at the diagram of a compass, you will notice that it shows 274° is actually a westerly direction.

Then if you use the latitude of approximately 24°S, which was placed inside that same envelope, and follow that to the east, it takes you to the Carnarvon Range in Queensland.

This envelope, with contents under seal, is only to be delivered to persons presenting an authority from me and signed as shown on margin hereof. It contains a record which is as near as possible correct, having regard to the unreliable nature of the scientific instruments used, of a rich gold bearing reef known to exist in the interior of Australia. Prominent landmarks are described and cross-bearings given on same. Compass bearings were taken by a compass which varied 274°E at Carnarvon in 1897

L H B Lasseter

Beatty

The front of the envelope that contained the bearings for the location of the reef, as signed by Lasseter and lodged with the Bank of Australasia before the CAGE expedition left Alice Springs in July 1930. (National Library of Australia)

Transcription of the front of the envelope:

'This envelope, with contents under seal, is only to be delivered to persons presenting an authority from me and signed as shown on the margin hereof. It contains a record which is as near as possible correct, having regards to the unreliable nature of the scientific instruments used of a rich gold bearing reef known to exist in the interior of Australia. Prominent landmarks are described and bearings were taken by a compass which varied 274° E at Carnarvon in 1897

LHB Lasseter'

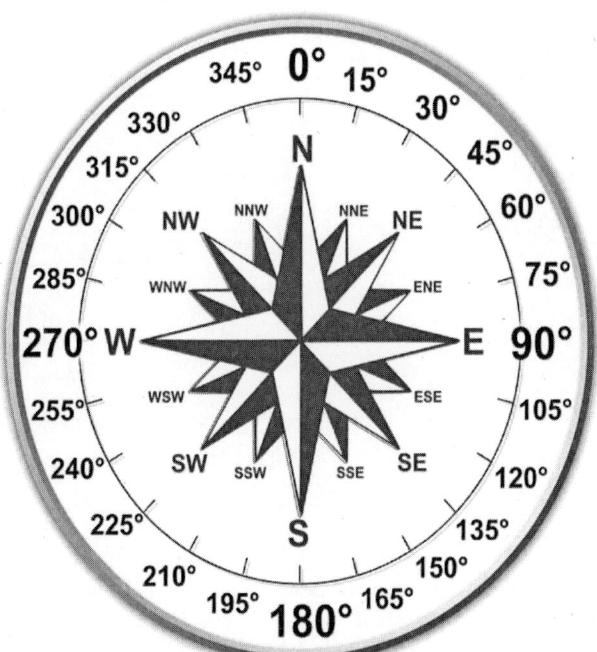

A compass clearly showing that 274° is a westerly bearing, not easterly.

Furthermore, if the bearing of 274°E at Carnarvon was used, it would have placed you at Spriggs, near Arltunga, where Harding successfully hid some of the stolen cattle.

Of course, when the compass bearing is applied today, allowances for the magnetic declination, or magnetic variation, need to be taken into consideration. So, if the original bearing was taken in about 1900 and we were to apply it in 2020, the magnetic variation would be between 5 and 7°, making the bearing somewhere between 279 and 281°. Either way, the bearing is still in a westerly direction and within the magnetic variation, therefore taking you to the exact same place, Spriggs.

This is all because Harding had originally taken the bearing east *at* Carnarvon, Queensland. Had Lasseter, whose completion of surveying and navigation certificates was always

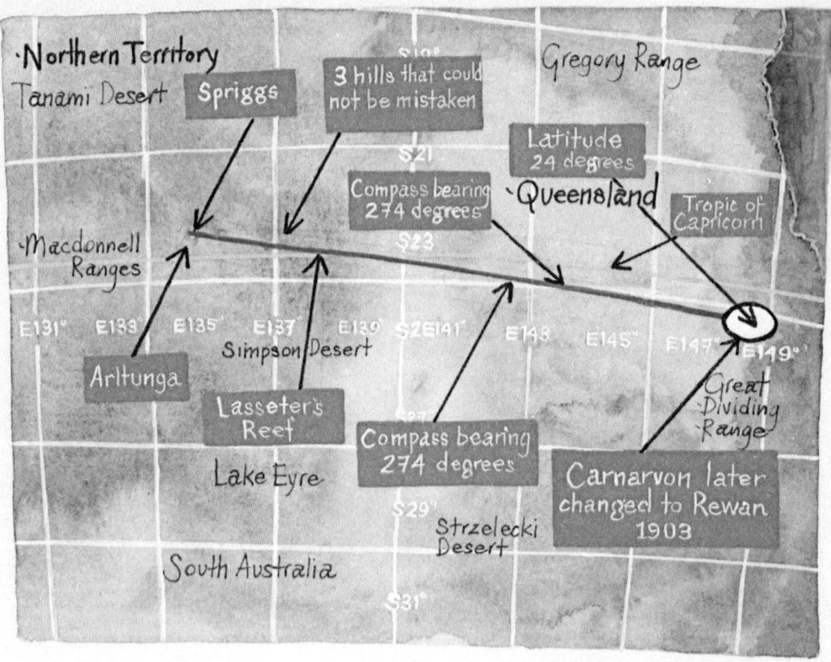

A map showing how the compass bearing of 274° runs between Spriggs in the Northern Territory and Carnarvon, Queensland. Note how the bearing falls in line with the three hills near the reef and the location of the reef itself. Although Joseph Harding could have taken that bearing at Carnarvon Station, Carnarvon Gorge or Carnarvon (all three fall in line with the bearing and were water sources), what is now known as Rewan has been used. (Belinda Williams)

questionable, known this about the compass bearing from the outset, he would have travelled in a westerly direction from Carnarvon in Queensland. No wonder he concocted the story about his and Harding's watches being out when he claimed that they'd relocated the reef. And no wonder aviator Charles Ulm said in the Sydney meeting that was held in 1930, before CAGE officially took flight, that the way Lasseter was describing the reef's whereabouts would place it in the Indian Ocean.

Even when I think back to the reconnaissance flight that Lasseter took with pilot Pat Hall over the Petermann Ranges during the expedition, when the landmarks are reversed, the equivalent range in the south-east is Mount Gardner. Although not as high as the Petermanns, it stretches from the Northern Territory and across the border into Queensland. It even has slightly similar contours. Again, it takes you directly to the reef in the east.

In January 1994, the exploration licence was finally issued to the syndicate, encompassing 150 square kilometres of the area on and surrounding the quartz-bearing reef. In the meantime, the quartz samples came back indicating that they, on average, assayed 2 grams of gold per ton. While Lasseter, courtesy of Joseph Harding, had claimed that previous samples assayed 3 ounces to the ton, I wasn't deterred. The samples that Michael, Lee and I had taken were from various spots on the reef, but given its enormity, it would be feasible that Harding's richer gold samples would have been taken elsewhere along it, or the needle as I call it, which we were still yet to find.

Furthermore, Lasseter had claimed that the samples he had were from a narrower section of the reef, which was about 3 to 4 feet wide. Aside from being where all of the landmarks could be clearly seen, after almost a century, this particular section of the reef, which could be where the mother lode is, is, as per the Dingo Dreaming, possibly buried by sand.

For me, though, the focus was to get the real story about Lasseter's Reef — the haystack — out there. However, another syndicate meeting decided that it was best to hold off. This time they were concerned that a large mining company would take over and rip us off. I was utterly disheartened. I reminded them that we had an exploration licence that covered the reef and an extensive area surrounding it. I also explained that we didn't have sufficient money to do it ourselves and we would need to engage an ethical mining company. Nevertheless, I was out-voted.

Six months later, I was relieved to be able to share the story about finding the reef, with the intention of gaining interest from a suitable mining company. In August 1994, I had an extensive feature in *People* magazine, which generated some interest. A few people contacted me, including a small group of businessmen from northern Australia. They had a mining company. Our discussions were promising — they were interested in backing the reef.

I also had a Queensland chap by the name of Doug Wilson track me down, after he, too, had read the *People* magazine article. Doug, who has an extensive background in doing the groundwork and acting as a consultant for mine geologists in remote parts of Queensland and the Northern Territory, explained to me that he had an interest in Lasseter's Reef. He'd read most of the books that I had and had studied several maps.

A couple of years before Doug contacted me, he had been approached by another fellow to help him find the reef. However, this other man's focus was closer to Western Australia. Doug told me that he didn't feel it was there, so declined the opportunity.

When Doug found out that I'd gone in the opposite direction and ventured to the east of Alice Springs, he said, 'It made all the sense in the world.' Once he and I had spoken about what my intentions were, he, along with a colleague from Mount Isa Mines, was keen to offer any advice if needed.

From then on, we continued to have many enlightening discussions on the phone. Doug was patient, intuitive and knowledgeable whenever we conversed, and he always asked thought-provoking questions. I learnt a lot from him.

Amid my excitement of being able to share how I found Lasseter's Reef and gaining interest in it, a fire went through the deli. A break in had occurred in the shopping centre where the deli was located, and a fire was subsequently started. Unfortunately fire and thick smoke had gotten into the roof, causing considerable damage.

Determined to rebuild, we put in an insurance claim. In the end, though, the insurance company wouldn't cover all of the costs to repair the deli, plus we discovered that some money had gone missing from the business. We had no other choice but to close it. Declaring ourselves bankrupt, we lost everything, including our two family homes, with my senior-aged parents living in one of them. At one stage, we were left with a few bean bags to sit in and ate tinned soups and noodles. We were practically homeless. Although immensely difficult, we decided to see our situation as an opportunity to start from scratch. What was important to me was that we had each other.

Despite all of this going on, I was still in contact with the northern Australian businessmen and Doug Wilson. We thought it was time to meet in person. With the syndicate's support, the members paid for my flight to Alice Springs in September 1994. I met with one of the businessmen at the local truck stop. He then drove us to the local caravan park, where I dropped off my swag. He was sleeping inside a cabin; I was sleeping on the firm ground and in the open air.

The next day, we drove out to meet with Doug Wilson, who was much taller and wirier than I'd imagined from our phone conversations, on the side of the road near Marqua Station. After a chat and a steaming mug of tea from the thermos, we drove out to the reef.

The purpose of this trip was to take further samples and to form a joint venture. While Doug agreed that I'd found most of the landmarks, he expressed one disappointment, especially in view of there being so much quartz throughout the area: 'Every geologist in the country who has ever gone across this part near the border would have seen this from the air, they would have seen and done something, such as rock chip it.'

'I don't think so,' I replied, shrugging my shoulders.

Then he added, 'To find a needle in a huge area of land with multiple quartz reefs, you're going to have to do a lot.'

But, after collecting various samples, talking at length, and staying overnight at the reef, on September 24 an agreement was signed, namely that the joint venture was 50/50 for the entire area that was covered by the exploration licence. Fifty percent was to go to the northern Australian businessmen. Furthermore, they would be responsible for renewing the exploration licence, which was due to happen within the next six months. The other 50 percent would be split between the syndicate, myself and Doug Wilson, which was known as the Decarli group on the agreement.

In the meantime, Doug kindly gave $5000 to the businessman to cover our flights and accommodation and for anything else that we needed to help us get going with the reef. However, I wasn't aware that Doug had done this at the time.

After we left the reef, the businessman drove us back to the caravan park, where, again, I slept outside under the shiny, pulsing stars. The following day, he dropped me off at the Alice Springs Airport. When I got back to Melbourne, a meeting with the syndicate took place, then the relevant documents were signed for the joint venture. It was around this time that I discovered that the businessman had used the $5000 Doug Wilson had given us for his own purpose. I advised the syndicate about this, but nothing more was said or done. I never received a reimbursement from him.

With the exploration licence about to expire in the first quarter of 1995, I made sure that everything was in place. But when I spoke with the businessman, he explained that the Department of Mines was going to renew the licence in his name as well as his other business partners. 'Seeing as we're doing all the work with the reef, we thought it'd be more appropriate that we receive 90 percent,' he said. 'I'm sure you understand, Bill.' Our original 50/50 agreement was no longer valid.

To clarify, this new agreement was for the northern area of the reef, which was the main area of interest. That would mean the syndicate, or Decarli group as it was known, would receive 10 percent for that area.

I then received a letter to confirm this new arrangement in writing. I wasn't particularly fazed, but it was a classic case of how gold creates extremes in people, namely greed and gold fever. My only disappointment was proving that Lasseter's Reef existed wasn't more contagious, especially since that has always been my focus.

With a new agreement in place, the exploration licence needed to be renewed as soon as possible. Despite the businessmen's assurances, and finally submitting the renewal, they missed the deadline — by twenty-four hours. Furthermore, Niche Explorations, a Queensland mining company, had put in a claim for the reef. Our grassroots syndicate had lost absolutely everything and had to dissolve.

I eventually made contact with Niche Explorations to pass on all the information that I'd collated about the reef. There was no point me hanging on to it. The two partners who formed Niche Explorations, Ian Fairbrother and Ian Smith, were most appreciative and came back to me a few weeks later, asking me if I would like to be involved as a consultant. I was stoked.

In 1995, some more samples were taken from the quartz reef. This time they ranged between 2 and 21 grams per ton. Overall, the area was proving to be quite gold and even silver positive. In addition, some opalisation has been found there, although the opal isn't commercially viable. Whenever we visited the reef, Niche Explorations was always considerate of the land and their practices, right down to how the portable toilets were used and where they were located.

When it came to drilling test holes in the reef, permission was required from the Aboriginal Areas Protection Authority. We then agreed to go out to the reef and meet with their representatives, to determine where the sacred sites were. After waiting for them for a few days, they didn't show up. Niche Explorations' director Ian Fairbrother decided that we may as well peg out the areas that we wanted to drill. Then, one day after the pegging was completed, the representatives from the Aboriginal Areas Protection Authority turned up. We were advised that all six of the pegged areas, which were predominantly near the three hills at Marqua Station, were on sacred land. We couldn't drill there.

Niche Explorations had already invested a significant amount of money and decided to let the Hay River mining licence go. Although hugely disappointing, I can understand why the area near the three hills is sacred. When I have visited there I have seen a circle of stones, old rocks that have been skilfully chipped into tools, and what appears to be a large rectangular window carved into a rock, possibly being a gateway into another dimension. In some ways, it could be an Aboriginal Stonehenge. Being among it is a deeply emotional experience, stirring a potent mixture of sadness, reverence and gratitude.

It also occurred to me that perhaps Harding knew all along that this particular section of the reef was a sacred site. The reason I say that is because when Lasseter wrote to Herbert Gepp in January 1930, by way of follow up to his previous correspondence, he believed, as shared in chapter 1, that the area was 'covered by the Aborigines reserve'. Now although Lasseter was doing his darnedest to get financial backing to the west of Alice Springs, and did actually go to Canberra to check if the area where he claimed the reef was, was sacred or not, I wondered if Harding had given him the heads up, despite it being to the east, all those years ago. At the time, a lot of that remote, arid interior in Central Australia was inhabited by Aboriginal people.

Still, I was determined to share the real story about Lasseter's Reef: it was time to prove its existence once and for all. Who else was willing to listen?

Chapter 12

On-Again, Off-Again

Swinging a large, heavy suitcase off the top of the bed, it landed with a loud thud on the floor. Despite taking almost fifteen years to compile pertinent and revelatory information about Lasseter's Reef, it only took me a day to pile every photo, document and map that I had about it into that big brown suitcase. Turning it side-on, I shoved it under the bedframe, well out of sight. By this stage, Pat, the kids and I had a place to rent, but I'd had a gutful of people who only seemed to want to know if the reef was laden with bloody gold or not, instead of the fact that Lasseter's Reef actually existed. It was time for me to relinquish my somewhat adventurous obsession.

It was also around this time that my thirty-one-year-old niece Corrina was in urgent need of having a kidney transplant. Despite her already having received a new kidney ten years beforehand (she was diagnosed with IgA nephritis at the age of seventeen), it had become diseased and was making her gravely ill. In addition to being on hemodialysis, she was constantly in pain. At one stage, she was in intensive care on a respirator. She could barely interact with her young daughter. It was heartbreaking to see her in that state.

As I was physically healthy and fit, I decided that I would donate a kidney to Corrina. After a series of tests and receiving approval to be a donor, the three-hour surgery, which saw me be peeled back like an orange to take my left kidney out, was conducted at Royal Melbourne Hospital in May 1995. Fortunately, Corrina felt much better than when she had her first kidney transplant, and continues to thrive to this day.

Within four hours of the operation, and with the assistance of a physio, I was up and moving around. A couple of months of recovery saw me bounce back with gusto.

In fact, I'd already started to take action about the lack of ambulance services in the Melton area before the transplant, given it was essentially a one-man service. Prior to the deli closing down, I had to drive an ambulance part of the way to the hospital, to meet an intensive care officer. My mum was in the back of the ambulance with acute respiratory failure. Since there was only one ambulance attendant in the area, he needed to attend to her in the back of the vehicle — she was deteriorating rapidly. He wasn't in a position to call the police or the fire brigade to get some assistance with driving it. Noticing how calm I appeared when he arrived to attend to Mum, he asked me to drive the ambulance instead. I didn't hesitate.

In the end, Mum was okay, but I started lobbying for services to be upgraded in the area. Melton was already isolated from essential metropolitan services such as hospitals. How was a one-man ambulance service going to cope with an ever-expanding residential area?

After garnering some attention in the local newspapers and attending meetings with representatives from the ambulance service and the council to provide input for improving services, the Melton ambulance service was eventually upgraded to a two-man crew.

Among all of this happening, I was surprised when I received a phone call from the producer at the *Bush Tucker Man: Stories of Survival* television series at the ABC. Hosted by Les Hiddins, a former Australian Army major who'd also spent time in the jungles of Vietnam, the producer was interested in sharing my discovery of Lasseter's Reef. Despite thinking that I was done with it, it was about three months after I'd donated my kidney to Corrina that I flew up to Alice Springs to meet with the production crew. From there, we headed out towards the reef to show how and where I'd discovered it.

This was my first time being involved with a documentary, and it was quite an eye-opening experience observing how the crew systematically worked together and still embraced those spontaneous moments. There was a lot of camaraderie and overall spending time with them was a lot of fun. However, when it came to me sharing my story about how I found the reef to the east of Alice Springs, Les didn't seem all that interested. On the one hand, he said to me that my research was 'impeccable'. It was a real compliment. On the other, he told me, 'This is one mystery I don't believe should be solved.'

I was baffled. I wondered why I was there at all.

Prior to the episode, titled "Gold Fever", airing in July 1996, I received a lovely letter from the ABC, thanking me for my input and participation. When it came to watching the program, Les essentially retold the story of how Lasseter had guided the CAGE expedition to the west and subsequently the south-west of Alice Springs, where he ultimately met his demise. Then, in the last few minutes of the episode, Les shared my name and a brief overview of my theory about how it was Harding who'd told Lasseter about the reef and that he'd potentially plotted the directions back to front. He also mentioned how Harding had lived in Arltunga, hence becoming aware of the quartz-bearing reef's existence. That I was thankful for.

However, while Les was talking to the camera towards the end of the episode, which was about 20 kilometres or so from where the three hills are at Marqua Station, he didn't sound convinced whatsoever about whether the reef existed or not. While we are all entitled to our opinions, he felt that it was Lasseter himself and the legend that he created that were most important, especially since Australia was such a 'young nation' and didn't have too many myths. Although I was disappointed with hearing this, Les, in his own way, helped share enough about my involvement with the reef to create further interest.

Shortly afterwards, I received a phone call from *The Great Outdoors* travel show at Channel Seven. I was flown to Sydney to meet with the producers and the program's host, Ernie Dingo, to discuss the idea of filming a story about finding Lasseter's Reef. Ernie didn't seem surprised about it being where I said it was. He agreed that it would be a cracking story. While it would be revelatory to many, in the end it wasn't considered suitable for a travel show, given people couldn't actually go and visit it. I was flattered that they'd asked and had taken the time to meet with me.

Even Eltham High School, my former secondary school, included a nice write up about me in one of their newsletters that year. I was touched, especially since I'd only been there for a few years.

Then *Australian Geographic* magazine was going to publish a story about me finding Lasseter's Reef. The write up had been completed and it was sent to me to check my quotes. But after I replied to confirm that all was fine, I received a phone call from them to say that I needed to provide 'irrefutable evidence' to back up my claims. They felt that there were some shortcomings with my version of events. I suggested that if they require conclusive evidence, they could fund the research for it. However, the editor indicated that they weren't in a position to do that. Neither was I. Wasn't the evidence the distinctive landmarks, especially since that was all Lasseter ever worked with, as well as share with the likes of Errol Coote? Nevertheless, the story was dropped.

Interestingly, in 1986, when *Australian Geographic* magazine was first launched by entrepreneur and explorer Dick Smith, it included an article on Lasseter's Reef. Smith had previously made attempts to find it. The first search was in August 1977 when he chartered a Qantas jumbo jet to take paying passengers on a ten-hour flight, which covered 5000 kilometres, over Central Australia. The 'arduous search' was accompanied by Bob Lasseter and Aboriginal tracker and artist Nosepeg Tjunkata Tjupurrula, who was thought to have witnessed Lasseter's death when he was about fourteen years old. Then, in 1985, Smith made another attempt to find the reef. Obviously both ventures were unsuccessful.

Even though my story hadn't been included in *Australian Geographic*, I still had people asking me about the reef and I continued to talk about it. I did what I could to further disprove myself, including reading just about every other book that had been written about Lasseter and his quest to find the reef, along with anything more I could find about Joseph Harding. There was nothing else I could do. People either believed me or they didn't.

In the meantime, everything I'd compiled about Lasseter's Reef was packed away in the suitcase and pushed back under the bed. It was only every now and then that someone would contact me, wanting to know some more information, so I would pull out the suitcase again to dig out photos and documents. Then it wouldn't go anywhere and I would put the suitcase back. I'd had enough; I was Lasseterered out. I thought that I would never go back out to the reef again.

CHAPTER 13
UNEXPECTED REUNION

The phone clicked loudly as I placed it back in the cradle. Here I go again, I thought, half-smiling and slowly shaking my head. Despite officially declaring to all and sundry that I wasn't going to entertain any more thoughts about Lasseter's Reef, like a boomerang, it reappeared in my life.

I'd just finished speaking at length with New South Wales based historian and author Edward "Ted" Wybergh Docker. He'd written a number of books, most notably the *Bradman and the Bodyline* series. Like so many others, Ted had read the *People* magazine article. He was fascinated with my discovery of Lasseter's Reef.

After some further discussions and briefly staying with us in Melton, he included my story in his book *Fabulous Furphies: 10 Great Myths from Australia's Past*, which was published in November 1997. It was both a joy and an honour to work with Ted. He was a pleasant gentleman. However, he was baffled that nothing further took place with Lasseter's Reef, particularly since I'd found the notable landmarks.

In between all of this, I started going to a psychologist. Although my sporadic relationship with Lasseter's Reef had taught me a lot about acceptance and letting go, the sessions helped me come to terms with how I'd approached things with my two children, Catherine and Anthony. I wanted to make contact with them, therefore I needed to take responsibility for my decisions and actions. I could no longer pin it on the Vietnam War.

After returning from the tragic futility of that war, I had intense anger, along with chronic insomnia and hellacious nightmares. I adored Catherine and Anthony, but at that young, impressionable stage of their lives, I thought it best if I wasn't around so much. I was too unsettled and didn't want to be a negative influence. I didn't want them to suffer.

After some in-depth discussions with their mother, Carolyne, and her new husband, Wolfgang, the gut-wrenching decision was made: I would no longer be a significant part of their lives. But I never anticipated that all contact would cease. Nor did I think that it would continue for what felt like an eternity.

It wasn't until I'd started doing the psychology sessions that I asked myself what the real reason was behind what I did. I realised that I'd become a victim of my own philosophy. It was also the beginning of understanding what post-traumatic stress disorder actually is. Again, Pat has been a tremendous support for me with all of this. If it wasn't for her, who knows what would have happened.

In 1999, I noticed that the *Herald Sun* published an article about Lasseter's Reef. The thrust of the story was about how the lost reef, if it did exist at all, was possibly somewhere to the west of Alice Springs. I contacted the newspaper and explained to the journalist, Kim Lockwood, how the reef wasn't there at all and that I'd actually found it back in 1991. After carefully listening to me and then asking me some detailed questions, Kim wholeheartedly believed that I'd found Lasseter's Reef.

By June, he had an article published in the weekend paper about my version of events, along with some comments from Ian Fairbrother of Niche Explorations.[1] It prompted more people contacting me, but not enough to get back out to the reef. Since Niche Explorations had surrendered the exploration lease for the Hay River, other people and/or organisations had taken on the exploration licence for that area, but it never amounted to anything. It was either too costly or they encountered roadblocks.

By 2000, Pat and I were starting to get back on board financially, even starting to save for our next family home. In between me dabbling with toy making, coming up with board game ideas and attempting to pitch them, I decided that I would at least write a book about the truth behind Lasseter's Reef. That way my journey with finding it was there for all to see, if they chose. As I mentioned in the Introduction, I co-authored the book *A Dead Man's Dream: Lasseter's Reef Found*, which was published in 2005. It generated more interest, with various articles being published, then it died down.

That same year, I was pleasantly surprised to receive a letter from a friend of Bob Lasseter's, Lister Ingham. Lister had intently followed the various expeditions searching for Lasseter's Reef. He wrote that after hundreds of unsuccessful expeditions to the west, he sincerely believed, like Doug Wilson, that the reef was real, it was just 'somewhere else':

> Your story just puts the skids under any thoughts they [the Lasseter family] had over the last many, many years ... I've looked at every idea put forward by various writers and you pick up flaws in every damn one ... I suggested that you, Dick Smith and Bob go for a trip in the area. What a good story to back up your work.

Lister also mentioned in the letter that after suggesting this to Bob, it was unlikely that he would hear from him again. Bob was so focused on finding the reef in the west.

Much to my astonishment, it wasn't long after the book came out that my daughter Catherine made contact with me. I was overcome with a mixture of joy and sorrow.

After gradually reacquainting ourselves over lengthy phone calls that sometimes continued until three a.m., and often finding it difficult to contain my elation that we had reconnected, Catherine and I decided to meet. I wholeheartedly welcomed her into my life, but also understood that she had questions and reservations about why I did what I did.

I suspect that she, like Anthony, felt angry and abandoned. The other incredible thing about Catherine and me coming together at this stage of our lives was that she and Anthony had their own families. I was a grandfather to three teenagers, namely Catherine's daughter Charli and Anthony's son Kyle and daughter Olivia. I was stoked to meet Charli and Olivia for the first time. I haven't met Kyle, nor reconnected with Anthony, but cherish the photos and updates that are shared with me.

Then, all of a sudden and for no obvious reason, things changed again between us. Relationships became strained. Catherine decided to break off contact. I understand that she has had her own challenges, so left her in peace. It was heart-rending. It was like connecting with them one minute, then having it wrenched away. I guess, in some ways, it was similar to what happened to Catherine and Anthony when they were young. Like Lasseter's Reef, they had disappeared from my life.

The following year, out of random curiosity, I did a search online to see who had the exploration permits for minerals, or EPM, as it is known in Queensland, for the Diamantina region. Located about 96 kilometres from where the Hay River exploration licence was, I figured that this area in Queensland was much closer to where Joseph Harding would have travelled while cattle duffing and had stumbled on the rich gold specimens from the reef. To my astonishment, no one had the EPM. It was available.

Excited, I rang Doug Wilson to see where he was at and what his thoughts were, especially since he had always been interested in acting as an advisor should anything ever eventuate with the reef. Equally jubilant, Doug said that he would get someone to secure the rights to the area as soon as possible. Not long after that, he sent me a letter saying, 'Sorry, we're too late. Another mining company has already got an exploration licence for it'.

Still, we decided to make contact with the mining company and spoke to the director, who was well regarded in the industry. He said that he would love for us join them out there at the reef. Everything was set. But the day before I was due to leave I received a phone call to say the trip had been cancelled. My heart sank. The director who I'd been speaking with was no longer there. Aside from the company going through some managerial changes in the lead up to the trip, apparently the company had already gone out there to do some unauthorised exploratory work, copping a whopping multi-million dollar fine in the process.

In 2011, an article was published in the *Australian* explaining how Dick Smith had purchased a map from eBay, showing what was believed to be the location of Lasseter's Reef.[2] Smith had purchased it from former North Sydney mayor Gerry Nolan, who had been a member of a geological survey party back in 1979, with the quartz outcrop, yet again, placed in the Petermann Ranges. Smith then flew out with Bob Lasseter to conduct a search based on this 'newfound' map. Although Smith claimed, in the article, to have found an enormous 'great reef' out there, like metallurgist Des Stroud, nothing more eventuated with the surface samples that were taken.

At the same time, filmmaker Luke Walker was in production with his documentary, *Lasseter's Bones*, which, fittingly, included Bob Lasseter's final journey to the desert, along with an appearance from Smith and a rather large and well-marked map. Authors Murray Hubbard and Richard Kimber also featured prominently in the film.

With Luke pursuing various lines of enquiry in relation to Lasseter and the reef, he contacted me and came over to the house to spend half the day filming with me and discussing my experience. I pulled out all the maps and the photos of the key landmarks that every Lasseter aficionado had been looking for, including Bob. They were clearly there to see.

Ironically, and not long after Michael and I had returned from our first trip in 1991, I had sent a letter and a video tape to Bob of the footage that I'd taken of the landmarks. A few months later, Bob kindly wrote to me and said that he thought he could see what I was getting at. However, at the end of the letter, Bob wrote that he 'could not ignore the evidence of my father's diary where he says "I have pegged the reef"'.

When it came to *Lasseter's Bones* being released in 2012, I went along with my son Daniel and a mate to see it. None of the filming Luke did with me made the final cut. Despite this, and the fact that it wasn't quite right from my perspective, there's no doubt that it was a terrific documentary. In fact, it went on to receive three nominations, including for Best Documentary at the Film Critics Circle of Australia Awards.

There were mentions of some other people in the film who seemed, at the time, to have played a minor role in Lasseter's quest to find the 'lost' gold reef. Most notably, it included the mysterious Swedish immigrant Olof Johanson, whom I mentioned in chapter 2, given he was to head out and meet Lasseter near Lake Christopher. In *Lasseter's Bones*, Luke had contacted Olof's Australian-born daughter Alvhild (Ann) Clark and includes the tricky phone conversation that he has with her. Not long after the documentary was released, she passed away.

While it was interesting that Luke had made contact with her, I didn't give a second thought about Olof's relevance at the time, mostly because I'd discovered that it was Joseph Harding who'd discovered the reef in the first place. I even rang Luke to congratulate him for doing a sterling job. However, I could hear in his momentary pause a combination of him being shocked and bracing himself before I continued. Perhaps he was expecting a rant from me, not praise. That said, the DVD of *Lasseter's Bones* did include me at the beginning of the deleted scenes. Regardless, it was time to let Lasseter's Reef go — again.

Without any purpose other than fun, I applied as a contestant on *Millionaire Hot Seat*. While the television quiz show's host Eddie McGuire was talking to me during my question time and finding out a bit more about me, I mentioned how I would love to have a meeting with Dick Smith so that he could prove me wrong about my theory of Lasseter's Reef. Not surprisingly, that too never made it to air. Neither did I lock-in the correct answer to the question.

The inconsistent interest with Lasseter's Reef and not having enough people share my enthusiasm has been the biggest frustration and disappointment. I also decided that if I'm going to have other people involved with the reef, they have to be the right people: they have to be genuine, open-minded and honest. They have to have the right intention. And, obviously, they believe that Lasseter's Reef exists. Otherwise, everything I've found has been a remarkable coincidence.

Clearly, there have been some people who have tried to prevent me from proving that Lasseter's Reef does exist, because if I do, it will only kill all of their stories. Nobody likes to look like a fool, and that's never been my intention. All I've ever wanted to do is put the record straight. It is a shame that everyone who has ever had an interest in the reef hasn't worked together. Then again, maybe no one really wants the whole mystery surrounding Lasseter's Reef to be solved.

Incredibly, in 2016, I received an email from a producer who worked with American reality adventure series *Expedition Unknown*, which airs on the Travel Channel. The show is hosted by Josh Gates, who happens to have a degree in archaeology. The production was coming to Australia to film a story about Lasseter and his fabled gold reef. They wanted to speak with me, given my unique version of events. I was so elated that I almost jumped off my chair and through the roof when I saw that email in my inbox.

The producers and research team were quite thorough, even flying me to Sydney so that I could do a presentation for them, to determine if they were going to include my story or not. They liked what they saw.

Within a week, I flew to Alice Springs to do the filming. One of the producers asked me, 'Since Lasseter had used Lake Christopher as a radial point when he was searching for the reef to the south-west of Alice Springs, was there an equivalent lake to the south-east?' Although I'd always focused on the landmarks surrounding the reef, especially the three hills in the north-east and the Quaker hat, it wasn't until this point that I realised that there was indeed a lake: it was Lake Caroline and it acted like a mirror to Lake Christopher.

In addition to the crew filming with me, they also filmed with Australian author, television presenter and cartoonist Warren Brown, who'd released his rollicking book *Lasseter's Gold* the year prior. Warren had done an immense amount of work retracing the steps of the CAGE expedition and bringing all of the expedition members to life. However, it was in the second part of the *Expedition Unknown* episode, also called "Lasseter's Gold" which aired in January 2017 that they shared how I found Lasseter's Reef and that Joseph Harding was the man who'd known about it from the outset.

When the filming took place, we approached the tip of the reef by helicopter on the western side of Marqua Station. Josh was staggered by the amount of quartz that was scattered throughout the sunbaked landscape and how it all formed part of a ginormous quartz-bearing reef. Even more remarkable was how Josh chipped away at some quartz on the surface of the reef, only to find a fragment of gold glinting in a small piece of rock. Although it wasn't much, nor from the section of the reef where Joseph Harding's rich samples would have originally come from, Josh, whose grin could rival that of a Cheshire cat, was convinced that this was indeed Lasseter's Reef.

Chapter 14
Misadventure

The sliding glass door to the local pawn shop whizzed open. As I stepped inside, preparing to scour the computer section for some electronic bits and bobs, the staff members' friendly, familiar faces beamed at me. Then suddenly peppy chatter about my appearance on the *Expedition Unknown* program gathered momentum faster than a willy-willy.

The last time I'd gone in there I'd jubilantly encouraged some of the staff to watch the show when they had the chance. Although I'd spoken about the reef with them beforehand, I didn't think that they would watch it. Even the business owner, Jason Faddoul, whom I had occasional chats with, had seen it. He, too, was elated with the fact that Lasseter's Reef existed.

Walking towards me, Jason, a bronzed, compact and muscular man of Lebanese descent, asked me, 'When are *we* going out there?'

I thought he was kidding. 'Yeah, right mate,' I replied, smiling and politely waving him off.

From then on, each time I went back into the store, Jason would appear with boundless enthusiasm, quizzing me about when we were heading out to Lasseter's Reef. My reply was the same, until one day when he phoned me and said, 'You don't believe me, but I'm dead-set about going out to the reef with you and getting involved. There's obviously some truth to what you're saying. I wanna help. What's it gonna take to convince you?'

I was dumbstruck. In all my years of searching and willingly sharing my knowledge of the truth about the reef, this was the first time someone had actually come to me and said that they wanted to fully back me up.

After that, Jason and I had several extensive discussions, where I explained what was involved with the quartz-bearing reef, its history, and the protocols that needed to be followed in order to go out there. In the meantime, Jason did his own research about Lasseter's Reef, and I happened to notice that the EPM for the Diamantina region was available. I rang Doug Wilson to let him know that I'd been having discussions with Jason and we then spoke about the possibility of the three of us going out to Lasseter's Reef.

By November 2018, Jason and I flew from Melbourne to Mackay to catch up with Doug and discuss what the next step was. Within four weeks, Doug obtained the first prospecting permit title. Then, on December 3, Jason and I were on our way back to Queensland to see Doug again. This time, though, all three of us were actually heading out to the reef.

I flew from Melbourne to Brisbane, then on to Mount Isa to meet Doug, while Jason and a pilot, Doug Pratt, had flown on a Cessna to Boulia. From there, the four of us took a reconnaissance flight around the area surrounding the reef, to see what was going on and what we would do over the coming week.

We decided that when we were going to return to the area the next day, we would go to where the large, expansive claypan was. We agreed that Doug Pratt and Jason would fly out there in the plane, while Doug Wilson and I would drive out to Tobermorey Station, which sits on the border of Queensland and the Northern Territory, to meet with the station owners and managers. Afterwards, we would drive down to the claypan to meet up with the plane and leave the vehicle there. Since Marqua Station is on the western boundary, the idea was that Tobermorey would be our new starting point so that we could fly in and out from Boulia with relative ease. It also meant that we were not encroaching whatsoever on the sacred site near the three hills.

However, as we were walking out from our accommodation at the Boulia Caravan Park at first light the next day, there was a sudden change of plans. Jason said he was keen to have the experience of driving in the Australian desert. He was going to head out to Tobermorey Station with Doug Wilson in the vehicle.

Although surprised, I said to him, 'That's fine, mate. Go for it.' It was his first time in the remote outback, and Doug Wilson, who knows almost every inch of this part of the country, was accustomed to the rugged driving conditions.

Before they left, I double-checked to make sure they had enough water and energy bars, of which there were about twelve, as well as sufficient fruit. The water needed topping up, which I did, despite Jason assuring me that they had plenty. They ended up having about 60 litres. I went to give Jason the satellite phone, but he insisted that they would 'have comms out there'. They also had a two-way radio and an emergency beacon in the vehicle. For me, it wasn't ideal that they didn't have the satellite phone. Nonetheless, I relented.

Doug and Jason set off in the four-wheel drive and I flew off with the other Doug in the Cessna to head out towards the claypan, near the reef. As the plane started to circle lower and prepare to land on the smooth, firm claypan, Doug said, 'We can't land there, there's not enough to land on.'

So we headed back to the aerodrome at Boulia, thinking that we would wait for Doug and Jason to return to the caravan park later that day.

While waiting, we tried contacting them on the two-way radio, given their mobile phones were out of range. There was no response. Over and over, we attempted to make contact. Still nothing. The sun was starting to go down and it wouldn't be long until nightfall was upon us. They didn't come back.

We had to wait, somewhat anxiously, until the morning before we could go out again in the plane. I barely got any sleep in the cabin that night, tossing from left to right, then back again, wondering where Doug and Jason were. The main thing that worried me was if the vehicle had tipped over, they wouldn't be able to get in contact with anyone. It doesn't take much to flip a four-wheel drive out in the back of beyond. Or, God forbid, one of them had been bitten by a snake while having a pit stop and they were stranded somewhere.

After a sleepless night, Doug and I went up again in the Cessna, searching the red, rippled earth for any sign of Doug and Jason. We spent several hours flying all around the area where they had headed off from and where they were due to arrive near the claypan, checking and re-checking. Aside from the landscape being dotted with mulga, cattle and the odd homestead, there was barely any indication of human activity out there. It was time to head back to Boulia.

But just as we were preparing to return, Doug said, 'We're running out of fuel. I'm going to have to land the plane, now.'

Gripping the seat of the plane tightly, I thought, shit, this is what all of these years with Lasseter's Reef have come to. Besides people's lives being at risk, it was starting to feel like the blunders that occurred with Lasseter and the CAGE expedition almost a century ago.

Fortunately, Doug landed the plane effortlessly on the bitumen end of the Donohue Highway, not far from an outback station, then parked on the side of the road. The owner of the cattle property, Sam Beauchamp who, as I found out, was a councillor at the Boulia Shire Council, happened to see us from the homestead, then came down to check if we were okay. After we explained that we were low on fuel, thanks to Sam, we were able to refuel the plane from a forty-four-gallon drum with a pump, which he brought down on the back of his vehicle.

Then, as we were preparing to get back onto the sealed section of the road, readying ourselves for takeoff, the plane jerked to an abrupt halt. When we got out, we saw that the front wheel had sunk into the sand on the side of the road. The plane was bogged.

After furiously digging like meerkats, we managed to, with considerable force, push the plane back out on the road. When we got back in, Doug fired up the engine and the propellers. After thrumming down the thin section of bitumen again to gather speed, on take-off, Doug swiftly tilted the plane to the right, then back again. He managed to just narrowly avoid hitting a road sign. But immediately after that, there was an almighty clunk. The left wing of the plane had clipped another road sign. Nevertheless, we were finally airborne.

After we landed back in Boulia, we waited a bit longer to see if we were going to receive any contact from Doug and Jason. Nothing. At the same time, we noticed that the tip of the plane's left wing had been taken clean off from hitting the road sign and there was a huge dent only inches from the fuel tank. While it eventually needed repairs, thankfully the Cessna was still operational.

By this stage, it had been more than twenty-four hours since we had seen Doug and Jason. It was time to report them as missing.

At the police station, I was asked a number of questions, including if Doug and Jason had a satellite phone. I replied, somewhat embarrassingly, 'I've got it.'

Puzzled, the police officer rubbed his chin with the palm of his hand, then asked, 'How come you've got it?'

I explained to him that I did try to give them the satellite phone, but Jason said that they didn't need it. I knew it was a stupid thing to do at the time, but reluctantly agreed. It was a big mistake on my part. I hadn't done an outback trip for some time and had slipped back into an everyday way of thinking. I'd become too lackadaisical.

Once the report was made, the police officer said that he wanted Doug and me to search along the Donohue Highway, so we went back out. This time, though, we ended up flying the wrong way. We were heading to Mount Isa. I realised this when I couldn't pick up the Donohue and cried out, 'This isn't the way we went!'

In a wide arc, Doug turned the small plane around and eventually managed to pick up the highway, but it was too far back from where we actually needed to be. We had missed Glenormiston Station and subsequently Tobermorey, the two key places that would have given us a better chance of spotting Doug and Jason from the air.

We continued to fly above the highway and then back around the area where we had all originally intended to go. Again, no sign of them. With only an hour of daylight left, we kept searching, pushing on, but we had to return to Boulia.

As the plane turned around, we both happened to glance at the fuel gauge: it had fallen to empty. Aside from flying in the wrong direction to begin with, we'd been so determined to find Doug and Jason that our minds had become muddled. Doug warned me that we may have to make an emergency landing. While considering whether to land or not, we could see Boulia's cluster of buildings punctuated with green trees in the distance. Praying like crazy that we would make it there, we landed safely at the aerodrome. Stepping off the plane, I almost dropped to my knees to kiss the warm tarmac. I'd never been so thankful to be back on terra firma.

While the last rays of the late afternoon sun glistened off the bitumen, I returned to the police station and told the police officer that we still hadn't found Doug or Jason. The police officer wanted us to go back out again in the morning. This time, though, we were bringing in the cavalry, so to speak. The plan was that Doug and I would fly out in the Cessna at five a.m. Two emergency helicopters were at the ready at the caravan park, as arranged by owner Scott Blacket and his father Frank, and another helicopter was prepared to take off from Mount Isa if needed. Meanwhile, the robust, four-engine Orion aircraft with thermal imaging, also from Mount Isa, was going to search the area in the early hours of the morning.

Everything was set. But just before five o'clock the next morning, I got a phone call from Jason. He and Doug were on their way back to Boulia. Thank Christ for that.

I raced outside to wave down the chopper pilots, Scott and Frank, who were preparing to take off. 'Stop, stop,' I yelled out, while vigorously waving my arms above my head. 'There's no need to go. Jason just called me and they're okay. They're on their way back now.'

However, the Orion aircraft had already gone out to commence the early morning search. Aside from the ground being too hot, they couldn't find them because they didn't know they were already driving back.

What happened to Doug and Jason out there? They'd been missing for almost two days.

Chapter 15
Off Track

Doug Wilson

When Jason said that he had changed his mind about who was going with who as the four of us were about to leave Boulia that first morning, I remember saying to him, 'Jason, more haste, less speed. Let Bill and me do our thing.' But he insisted that he was going with me in the vehicle and that Bill was to go with the pilot. He wanted us to do the groundwork.

In spite of me preferring to work to my already marked maps, including where creeks and crossings are, and using my bush sense, such as remembering service tank locations, Jason plugged the coordinates into his GPS. He may have been well meaning, but when driving in the outback regions, like we were, you have to have a strong awareness of the desert conditions. Out there, the ground talks to you, particularly when you work with maps.

After we stopped at Tobermorey Station, at the Plenty Highway end to fill up with fuel and with the intention of meeting the owners, we discussed which way was best to go to meet Bill and Doug. As we couldn't go along the main station road, we had to go down along the road near the border of Queensland and the Northern Territory, which Bill had previously indicated to Jason, based on someone else's suggestion, was fine to do.

Straight away, Jason was keen to drive. However, I warned him that driving in this kind of country is completely different. It's pretty wild out there.

Sure enough, within the first few minutes of him driving, everything in the back of the vehicle got tossed around. We were jouncing over some pretty rough and sandy terrain. So much so, the water containers and equipment got thrown about and dislodged in the back of the vehicle. After pulling over to the side of the road to repack and secure everything, I said that I would drive from then on.

We had some punishing places to drive through, most of which could only ever be done at 5k's per hour. The slow-going pace and jostling around in what appears, to some, to be a waste landscape, became trying for Jason. Yet for me, this land is everything.

Understandably, as Jason was a first-timer in the outback, it wasn't something he was used to. Sometimes he would suggest, based on his GPS, that we go another way, but I would always encourage to first walk it. When we got out at one point, there was a rocky slope with steep edging. It was impossible to get down and I knew that if we attempted it, we would never, ever get out. I explained to Jason, 'Two things could happen. One: we could roll over if we go down there. Or two: we won't be able to reverse up. It's too risky. We are not going down.'

So we continued going back towards the way I was more comfortable with. I recalled seeing a road that would take us back to Boulia and suggested to Jason that we return there to regroup and reorganise ourselves. He said that since we were already out there, he didn't want to go back. He wanted to keep heading in the direction of the reef. Jason figured that if we took another road, he would then be able to pick it up on his GPS, which would, ideally, take us back around to where the plane was due to land.

Although Jason was directing me with the GPS, intuitively I knew that the road I had suggested would lead us back to the main highway. I was feeling uneasy about where we were going. Sure enough, we came to a river and Jason said, 'If we can get across to the other side, there's a road that'll take us 'round to where we want to go.'

When we got to the river crossing, it had been washed out. Concerned, I said, 'I think we should stay on this side of the river and sit on the road 'til morning.' So we did. We slept overnight in the car.

The following morning, aside from figuring out exactly where we were, Jason was still eager to find *the* road on the other side of the river. The plane hadn't flown across us as anticipated, we hoped nothing was wrong. So we drove a bit further along and down into the river. I explained to Jason, 'We can get out of here but I'll go and walk the track for a little bit to pick the best way.'

While I walked around surveying the area, Jason hopped back into the car and started driving along the sandy riverbed. Throwing my hands up in the air, I wondered what the heck he was doing, especially since I wasn't quite ready to decide where we should go across.

He wasn't even at the steering wheel for a minute when he ploughed headlong into a gully filled with fine, dry sand, just before our way out of the river. We were stuck — and in scorching 45 degree heat.

I dashed over to the car. Jason explained that he thought he was helping by driving up a bit further to get a clearer view of what was beyond the surrounding hills and dunes. He then hopped out of the driver's seat and I jumped into it to reverse the car back a little, to see if we could take a different angle, but the wheels had no traction. The vehicle sank even deeper into the soft sand.

I then worked all day, on my hands and knees, digging the vehicle out. Jason, to his credit, did the best he could, but struggled with the stifling heat and swarms of flies. He wasn't acclimatised to the desert and had to go in and out of the vehicle to cool off with the air conditioning. Although we needed to conserve as much fuel as possible, there is no point fighting it when things get too challenging out there: the desert will always defeat you. The only way we were going to get out alive was to dig ourselves out. That was my sole focus.

Later in the day, I was amazed when Jason said that he was going to walk 15 kilometres to where he believed was a station house. But I was aware that it was nothing more than an old converted shed in the middle of the desert. There was nobody there to help. As frustrating as it was for him, I urged Jason not to go there. If he did, he would have died in the desert, just like Lasseter. Although Jason was almost out of cigarettes and needed to call his contacts, he agreed not to leave the vehicle as we already had supplies.

It was just on the edge of darkness when I was finally able to reverse the vehicle back a little so that we could then drive it out. After twelve onerous hours, we were mobile again, but Jason still wanted to find this particular road. I believed that we needed to go back the way I was familiar with. Eventually, we did. From there, Jason's GPS picked up the coordinates. He agreed that the road we were on would take us past Glenormiston Station. Strangely, it was the same road that we were on the night before, only further up, and it took us to the Donohue Highway. This time, we were on our way back to Boulia.

When we arrived there, we saw the helicopters, police and a couple of four-wheel drives waiting for us, ensuring we were safe and well. I was beyond relieved to be back and that the rest of the search party didn't have to go out looking for us.

After more than fifty years of crossing the central Australian desert, it was the first time in my life that I had been lost. I regard myself as a humble man at the best of times, but was even more so. I was deeply embarrassed. All I could put it down to was human error. An incorrect coordinate had been entered into the GPS at the outset and we had taken a wrong turn after we stopped at Tobermorey. Combine that with Jason's unfamiliarity with being in such extreme conditions and, for my part, allowing us to get into that dreadful situation. I didn't listen enough to my bush sense. I didn't listen to the land. Never before had I relied on GPS bush road navigation, only my pre-journey mindset maps. However, this time I dropped my guard and believed the GPS.

The following day, after everything had settled down, Jason came up to me. Putting his hand on my shoulder, he said, 'I now understand how harsh and challenging it is out there. I'll remember being stranded in the desert for the rest of my life. And I'd never have gotten outta there if it wasn't for you.'

I was grateful for him acknowledging that.

Jason Faddoul

For most of my childhood, I grew up in the country, at Ararat, in south-west Victoria. Like Bill, I've always had an adventurous spirit. I'm a risk taker. But since this was my first time in the outback, I didn't know what to expect out there. As odd as it sounds, being stuck way out in woop woop with Doug, especially since he's been exposed to that kind of country for most of his life, was an insane experience and I wouldn't change a thing.

The day before we got bogged, we'd been driving further into the desert. There was a turning point after we'd left the main part of Tobermorey Station: we could go left, straight ahead or right. We chose left. That's what took us completely off-track — 'round and 'round a giant mountain that only seemed to get higher and go on forever. We even tried going over it. It drove us friggin' crazy.

Although we ended up being miles from where we were meant to be, our biggest worry was that we hadn't seen the plane with Bill and Doug fly over us. I hoped to hell it hadn't gone down.

As for me getting the car bogged down in a gully, when I first jumped into the vehicle at about six or seven a.m., I thought that I knew what I was doing. How hard can it be to drive 100 metres?

Even the shovel, which had been packed in the vehicle before we left, was lost. The night before, while we were parked on the side of the road, Doug needed to relieve himself, so he grabbed the shovel out of the back of the car to dig a hole. When he came back, he left the shovel on top of the vehicle. After he got a couple of hours' kip, we started driving again at about two a.m. Later that morning when the car got bogged, Doug went to get the shovel, but it wasn't there. It'd fallen off when we left in the dark hours of the early morning.

While Doug worked like a disciplined soldier to dig us out, the heat was so disgustingly brutal it sizzled my brain, making me hallucinate. From the middle of the day, I'd slog up to the top of the hill about every thirty minutes, with my tired, burning eyes constantly searching for the plane. I was praying so much for it to come over and find us, but mostly to know that Bill and Doug were okay.

Sometimes I'd yell out, 'Doug, I think I can hear the plane!'

But my ears were deceiving me. It was just the wind blowing through the trees.

Time dragged so slowly in that godforsaken place. I just wanted to get out of there. With no mobile phone coverage and a dead two-way radio, I stared at the emergency beacon: should I press the button or not? I tried to talk Doug into pressing it. At first, he didn't wanna touch it. He said, 'We don't need help. We'll be fine.'

By four o'clock, I begged Doug, 'We've only got a few hours of light left. I don't want people worrying about us, plus we don't know what's happened to Bill and Doug. We have to press the button, now!'

So I did. There was no sound, no sign, no nothing. For about an hour and a half, I kept pressing the emergency beacon, in between looking up to the big blue sky, hoping someone would find us soon.

Suddenly I thought I saw something with wings, like a glider plane, coming towards us, then vanish. It'd reappear and disappear. My eyes were playing tricks on me. No one came.

It took a while, but we realised the emergency beacon hadn't been activated when the car was hired. Then, in the last hour, Doug got a small tree to jack up the front left wheel from the outside. That's what got us outta that rut.

***

As much as Lasseter's Reef has been a significant part of my adult life, I had to be honest about the reasons why Doug Wilson, Jason and I were in the outback. This was my eighth visit to the area since 1991 and now two lives had been put at risk. What was more important, putting a stake in a claim for a supposedly rich gold-bearing reef that has been part of Australian mythology and folklore for almost a century, or ensuring that people were safe, alive and well? To me, their lives are far more important than anything else that may be out there. I don't believe in achieving anything at any cost.

Surprisingly, after we found out where Doug and Jason had gotten stranded, we realised that they were actually within about 92 kilometres of the reef, but because the sand dunes were so high, with some being up to a staggering 10 metres, it was difficult for them to get across country. They were actually closer to Carlo Station on the Queensland side. And if they'd taken the main road, which was the longer but more accessible way around, they would have been about 160 kilometres away from the reef.

What was also interesting was how Scott Blacket, from the Boulia Caravan Park, had mentioned that he'd spoken with a local chap by the name of Phillip Anderson about our reasons for being in the area. It ultimately led to Doug Wilson having an intriguing chat with Phillip. His grandfather, Robert Anderson, first established Tobermorey Station in about 1913. Then, Phillip's father, Alexander "Scotty" Anderson, was born at Tobermorey and, as an adult, eventually moved across to manage the neighbouring Manners Creek Station, which used to form part of the one property.

When Phillip was growing up, he clearly recalls his father, who has since passed away, telling him that it was while he was still working at Tobermorey Station that the Aboriginal people who were living there would sometimes go walkabout for a week or two. They would often head down south towards the area we'd just started exploring; somewhere along the line of the ironstone quartz reef. Then, Phillip's father would see the Aboriginal people come back with rocks of native gold, or what they called 'pretty rocks'. He figured that if they were bringing in rocks of gold, there had to be a rocky reef with some gold in it somewhere nearby. When the Aboriginals were asked where they got the gold rocks from, they would usually say that it was 'from a two- or three-day walk down that way'. After they brought the gold in, the white fellas would then exchange things like sugar, flour or tea for it. To the Aboriginal people, these items were far more practical.

Of course, once Lasseter's story became the talk of the nation, especially in the books and articles that came out in the 1930s and 1940s, Phillip's father made the connection between the reef and the fact that he used to see the Aboriginal people coming up from Tobermorey with the gold rocks. Later on, he made the comment to Phillip that the reef was to the east of Alice Springs. He knew that unless any of the expedition members, especially Lasseter, were clued-in prospectors or miners, or even ex-army members, who understood how maps were often coded or reversed to hide something of value from the enemy, they would never find it over to the west. They were looking in the wrong place. But no one ever took any notice of what Alexander Anderson said. Until now.

After having a couple of days to regroup, Doug Wilson and I arranged to fly by helicopter from Boulia to a small section of the reef with Scott Blacket, while Jason and Doug returned to civilisation. Although it was exhilarating to finally put our feet back on the reef after another hiatus, our focus was to do some rock sampling and obtain more bearings.

Bizarrely, something else occurred to me while we were out there in that hot, dry and dusty December: it was about the same time of year that Lasseter had claimed to have gone across from Queensland via Cloncurry, be it 1897 or whatever year he decided that he went. Although I've already determined that Lasseter never went out into the desert before the CAGE expedition, but instead based his claim on where Joseph Harding had been and what he'd told him, this was the first time that I had attempted to approach the reef from the north-east. In other words, I'd travelled down from Mount Isa to Boulia, then headed across to the reef. Therefore, I was closer to many of the places that he had mentioned. My skin tingled at the thought. Were we getting closer to the mother lode — the needle?

Chapter 16
In Threes

It is said that every number has its own symbol or meaning. I'm not a particularly religious person, but the number three is often referred to in the Bible as a completion. Other interpretations say that it refers to having a strong sense of faith, wisdom and guidance; that patience is required; to expect the unexpected.

When I went on my first trip to Lasseter's Reef in 1991, I mentioned how I noticed a constant theme of the number three occurring. I didn't know what it meant at the time, but sometimes wondered if it related to the three hills, which ended up being part of the area that is declared sacred. In January of 2019, Doug Wilson, Jason and I flew out to the reef by helicopter, especially since Jason didn't actually set foot on it the month beforehand. Aside from the misadventures of that December trip, the surface samples that were analysed weren't quite what we wanted. But the three of us were mainly there to celebrate.

By this stage, the exploration permit for minerals (EPM) for the quartz-bearing reef had been applied for. It usually takes about twelve months to be officially granted. We had, at least, become approved applicants. At the same time, Jason formed a company, namely B.S.T Explorations, with BST standing for Blood, Sweat and Tears. Besides representing almost forty years of unstinting effort with Lasseter's Reef, when I was in the army, I was in the 31 section, which had a call sign of blood (for the command vehicle), sweat (for the alpha vehicle) and tears (for the bravo vehicle). My daughter Alycia thought it appropriate to name the company after that.

In addition to Jason being the director, Doug and Alycia have become shareholders in the company. Like I have always said, it has never been about the gold for me. I guess I'm more of a caretaker.

And just when I thought I'd found all of the key elements and indicators to prove that Lasseter's Reef existed, incredibly some other lesser-known pieces fell into place. At the time of writing this book, writer Kristin Lee encouraged me to read the book *Olof's Suitcase*, written by Australian military historian Chris Clark. After the *Lasseter's Bones* documentary came out in 2012 and included the phone call with Olof Johanson's daughter, Alvhild Clark, Chris was compelled to research and write the book, especially since Alvhild was his mother and Olof was his Swedish grandfather. Prior to the documentary going into production, Chris was unaware of his family connection to Lasseter's Reef.

As discussed in chapter 3, Lasseter, while haphazardly and somewhat deliriously writing notes to his wife Rene during his final months in the central Australian desert, first made mention of Johanson (various spellings of his surname occur in different accounts) in his diary. He wrote that the prospector, who happened to be working in Kalgoorlie-Boulder, Western Australia, knew of the reef's location:

> Also it was agreed upon Fred Blakely when I ... engaged to go with the camels that if I did not show up again by the end of November that they would send a man named Johansen to my relief. As I believe he also stumbled on to this identical reef I had to go right out to Lake Christopher which is 100 miles across the WA border in order to get my bearings, then I was [indecipherable — able?] to go direct to the reef.[1]

However, if Fred Blakeley, as Lasseter stated, did know about Johanson, why didn't he mention it in his book *Lasseter's Dream of Millions*, or any other of his documentation relating to the CAGE expedition for that matter? When it came to Lasseter, Blakeley, ultimately, was fairly blunt. It seems, as author Des Clacherty shared in his book *On Lasseter's Trail* that the letter Lasseter gave to Paul Johns to deliver to the Government Resident at Alice Springs, which Errol Coote claimed to have seen, was the first hint about Johanson:

> In the letter, Lasseter said that he had been to the reef and now planned to go to Lake Christopher to meet Johannson ... The mention of Johannson came as a surprise to everyone as his name had not been heard before by the expedition members in Central Australia. How Lasseter had made that arrangement for the meeting is still a mystery.[2]

Not surprisingly, the letter to the Government Resident was never found.

However, there was more correspondence between Lasseter and Johanson than first thought, which author Billy Marshall-Stoneking included in the second edition of his book renamed *Lasseter: In Quest of Gold*. For starters, on 16 June 1930, a telegram, which Bob Lasseter has had in his keeping, was sent from Johanson while he was in Coolgardie, Western Australia, to Lasseter's home address in Kogarah, New South Wales. Not only was this sent before the CAGE expedition commenced, the contents of the telegram indicated that it was in response to a letter Lasseter had sent him.[3]

In addition to the telegram, a three-page letter dated 23 July 1930 was written by Johanson, this time when he was in Boulder City. Based on the contents, he seemed to be responding to Lasseter's concerns about the possibility of the Aboriginals launching an attack, as well as clarifying the description about Lake Amadeus, further proving that Lasseter had never set foot in Central Australia beforehand.

However, Lasseter never saw that letter because he was already on the expedition in Central Australia. What's also interesting about all of this is, Johanson's written

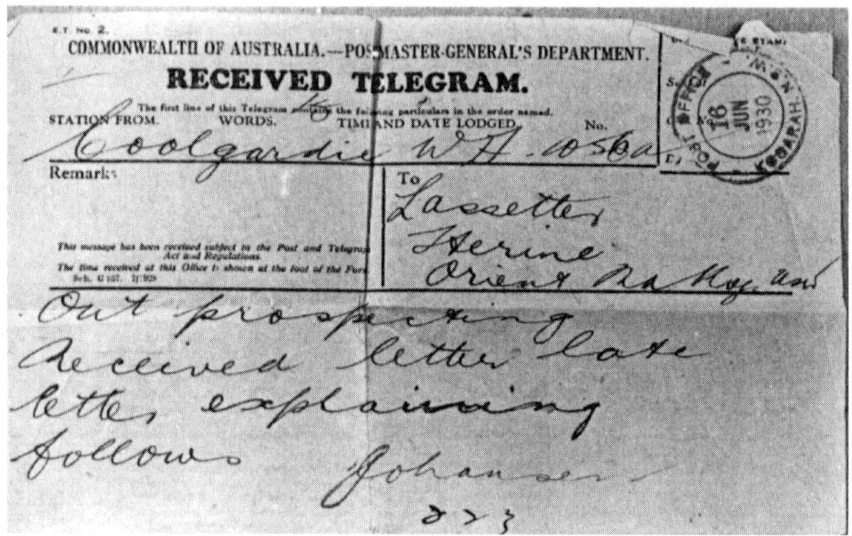
COMMONWEALTH OF AUSTRALIA.—POSTMASTER-GENERAL'S DEPARTMENT.

RECEIVED TELEGRAM.

STATION FROM. WORDS. TIME AND DATE LODGED. No.

Coolgardie W.A.

Remarks

To Lassetter
Herine
Orient Rd Kogarah

Out prospecting
Received letter late
letter explaining
follows
Johansen

POST OFFICE 16 JUN 1930 KOGARAH

Olof Johanson's telegram to Lasseter, June 1930, confirming that he received Lasseter's letter and to expect a written reply. (Courtesy of Bob Lasseter)

correspondence to Lasseter is what eventually became evident. Yet the written correspondence from the ever-elusive Lasseter to Johanson never transpired.

Even the fact that Johanson mentions in that same letter that he received written correspondence from John Bailey, asking him to be on standby to join the expedition, shows that Lasseter and Johanson were definitely acquainted before the expedition took place. But how did they come to know each other?

Based on Chris Clark discovering that Johanson sailed from Sweden and arrived in Adelaide in August 1914 and then married there in 1923, I realised that this was the same time that Joseph Harding was residing there. And then, of course, Lasseter, as I said in chapters 7 and 9, was working in Adelaide, including his short stint in the army, and convalescing from his head injury in 1917. While Johanson moved between Adelaide and various regions of South Australia for work between 1916 and 1921, which was partly during World War I, he was required to lodge a Notice of Change of Abode with the police every time he changed residence.

Olof Johanson in Adelaide, August 1918. (Image courtesy of Chris Clark)

According to the Notice of Change of Abode that Johanson signed on 14 December 1917 and the Form of Application for Registration signed on 14 December 1916, his residence was 97 Flinders Street, Adelaide.[4] He was living smack-bang in the city. Therefore, all three men were in Adelaide in 1917, and somehow Joseph Harding had shared his story with Lasseter and Johanson.

As for how they may have connected, it is possible that they'd all attended the same event or taken the same bus. Or had they met at the Adelaide Botanic Garden, an oval or the zoo? They could have randomly met at a local watering hole. Perhaps Harding and Lasseter had met first, followed by Johanson, or was it vice-versa? There are numerous possibilities. Regardless, it didn't change the fact that it was

Harding who knew about the reef in the first place. It only reinforced it.

We already know that in 1917, Joseph Harding was living at his niece and nephew's residence at Torrensville. And although Lasseter noted his usual place of residence as Port Adelaide, his sister Lillian lived at College Park. Then, of course, with Johanson living in Flinders Street, he was the most central. No matter how they may have intersected, these residences were in remarkably close proximity to one another. Therefore, they could have met on the side of a street.

Let's not forget that Harding was well-known around Torrensville, especially since he was regarded as the last of the old-timers from Central Australia, while Lasseter was known to regale people with his tales. One could have heard about another and then sought them out.

Regardless of how they met, Johanson and Lasseter had both interpreted Harding's detailed recollections of the lucrative gold-bearing reef to the west of Alice Springs, not to the east. As we are aware, Harding died in January 1928.

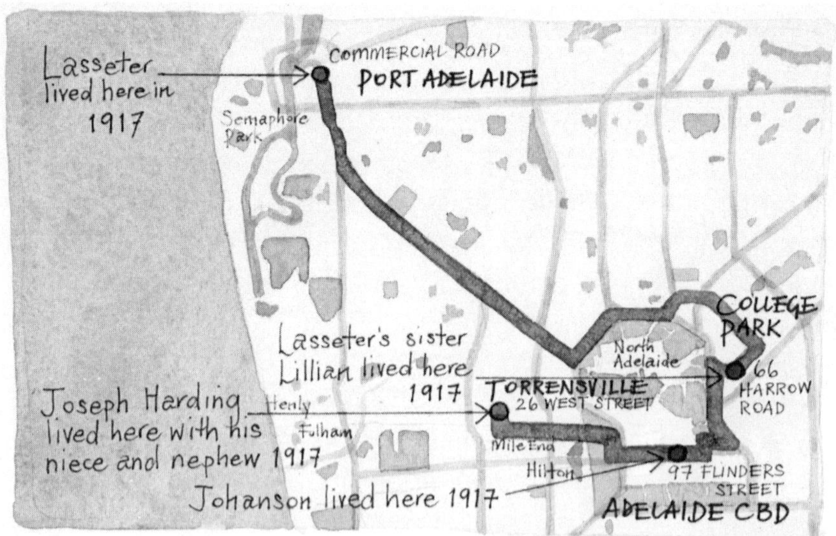

Close quarters: the location of the residences of Harold Lasseter, Joseph Harding, Olof Johanson and Lillian McGrath (Lasseter's sister) in Adelaide, 1917. (Belinda Williams)

Was an arrangement made between Johanson and Lasseter, whereby Lasseter was the front man to find a backer to fund an expedition to the reef as of 1929? And if things got challenging, as they did with the CAGE expedition, was Johanson to come to his aid, or, as he suggests in his letter to Lasseter, act as guide?

Even though Johanson was working in Western Australia as of October 1929, what's particularly interesting about this timing is that it was in mid-October of that same year when Albert E. "Texas" Green, the Minister for Defence, received the letter from Lasseter, regarding his discovery of an enormous gold-bearing reef. Had Johanson gone out there to deliberately scout the area to the west of Alice Springs in preparation, then work in the goldfields until Lasseter had found a financier?

It seems, based on photos that Chris Clark had found in Johanson's suitcase in Sweden that Johanson was already working in Central Australia between 1928 and 1929 before heading to Western Australia. An even more astonishing revelation was how these photos were further supported by personal papers of Neville Wolff with whom Johanson worked with in Kalgoorlie in 1929 and 1930. In them, Wolff claimed that Johanson told him that while he'd been out dingo-hunting in Central Australia, he'd accidentally stumbled on a reef. In his version, though, an old shallow shaft had been sunk on it. Perhaps Johanson was trying to get an even bigger head start.

Then when Lasseter met Bailey at the AWU in 1930, did he make mention of Johanson? If he did, it is likely that Bailey may have said, like he did about Harding had he known about him, that it was more believable to only publically announce that Lasseter had found it.

Then again, it is thought that Johanson, a member of the AWU, had written a letter to the union after an article about Lasseter and the proposed CAGE expedition was published in Perth's *Daily News*. In it, Johanson also claimed that he knew where the reef was. If that was the case, why hadn't he at least pegged it? It is far more likely that the letter was a deliberate ploy to further convince Bailey that the reef existed.

As we know, the entire CAGE setup reeked of greed-driven deception, and there's no doubt that Bailey was covering all of his bases. Therefore, he must have made secret alternative arrangements with Lasseter and Johanson, only to alter them to suit his own agenda.

Even before Lasseter went missing, Johanson and his prospector companion with the name of John Jackson Smith had already commenced their own expedition, having travelled by train from Western Australia to Alice Springs in September. They had, presumably courtesy of Johanson sharing his letter to Lasseter with his Western Australian mine employers, the backing of what became known as the "Pieterman [sic] Gold Mining Syndicate". It seems that they wanted to find it before the CAGE expedition. During their almost four-month journey, Smith recorded his and Johanson's various encounters in a diary while scouring the south-western region of Central Australia, particularly around the Petermann Ranges, when they eventually got there.[5]

But while travelling to Ayers Rock (Uluru), and then on their return to Alice Springs in the first half of December, they never came across Lasseter, who ultimately perished in the desert. Nor did they find the reef. Like Lasseter, Johanson couldn't recall its location.

Interestingly, while Johanson and Smith were making their way back, Smith mentioned in his diary that the pair had tea at Bob Buck's station, Middleton Ponds.[6] The world only gets smaller.

In 2019, Chris Clark released another book. Titled *The Truth About Lasseter*, the well-researched book goes into great detail about Lasseter's life, from beginning to end. While Clark concludes, like me, that Lasseter never found the reef, he also claims that the reef doesn't exist. He is right: the reef doesn't exist to the west of Alice Springs, but as I have outlined in this book, and based on all of the evidence that I have found, it is to the east!

Another interesting detail Clark mentions, based on an article published in Sydney's *Daily Guardian* newspaper in January 1931, is how Lasseter's wife, Rene (referred to as Irene in Clark's book), was already aware that Johanson was employed by another company to find the reef since August 1930, while her husband, who was somewhere out in the arid heart, wasn't. She and John Bailey, who was undoubtedly across this, too, had no way of giving Lasseter the heads up.

As Clark suggests, Rene's knowledge must have arisen from seeing and then replying to Johanson's letter to Lasseter in July 1930, with her indicating that Lasseter had departed for the CAGE expedition. Realising that he'd been double-crossed, Johanson promptly sought backing elsewhere. It is even possible that he replied to Rene, advising of his intentions.[7]

After returning from his and Smith's failed expedition, Johanson made another attempt, this time with a man named Tracy, to relocate the reef the following year from the Western Australian side. Again, he came back empty handed.[8] Understandably, Johanson wanted to lie low. After working various jobs in Adelaide, then Melbourne, he eventually returned to Sweden in about 1948. He died there seven years later.[9]

CHAPTER 17
AS GOOD AS GOLD

I couldn't believe what I was seeing. 'Wow that looks like the head of a sphinx!' I exclaimed to Doug Wilson while pointing out of the front left passenger window of the car. Clearly within our view for about thirty seconds was an unusually tall and erect rock feature sitting atop a hill, with its base looking more like a triangulated mound.

Doug and I were driving from Mount Isa to Boulia on our January 2019 trip to head out to the reef with Jason in the helicopter. It was just before the small, remote town of Dajarra that I noticed the striking red-orange rock formation, otherwise known as The Monument.

Despite Doug having driven past it many times before, it wasn't until I pointed it out that he agreed that it looked like a sphinx. Not only was it the first time that he'd looked at it from a different perspective, it was the first time that I'd ever seen it. This was, after all, only the second time I'd travelled from that direction to go to the reef.

But it wasn't until a couple of months later that I realised what this conspicuous looking rock actually meant. During the research of this book, writer Kristin Lee watched the *Lasseter's Bones* documentary. She noticed that while Bob Lasseter and Luke Walker were somewhere out in the irrepressible desert to the west of Alice Springs, Bob recalled the various key landmarks (most of which I'd already found), wondering if he and Luke could see them, in some way. Not surprisingly, they didn't.

When Kristin heard Bob mention that he was trying to find something that looked like a pharaoh's head and what could possibly represent an outline of a child climbing a mountain, she phoned me and asked, 'What's this pharaoh's head that Bob Lasseter is talking about?'

Although pharaoh's head is written on one of the pictures in Lasseter's Diary, it wasn't something I'd previously paid much attention to, nor had many of the other accounts that have been documented over the years.[1] It was only when Kristin asked me that question, my mouth opened wide in amazement as the connection suddenly dawned on me: I'd inadvertently discovered, with my own two eyes, another landmark for Lasseter's Reef.

Depending on which way you look at it, on one side it looks like a sphinx, or a pharaoh's head, and on another it can appear to be an outline of a child climbing, although some have even said it could look like a bird, perhaps a galah. Either way, there are definitely physical looking features, especially what appear to be eyes watching you, as well as a nose and hands, although they could be paws or claws. Given that Joseph Harding was often moving cattle to Dajarra, he would have clearly seen this too, hence why it was noted in what became Lasseter's Diary.

Of course, in ancient Egypt, a sphinx was a mythological creature, with the body of a lion and usually the head and/or headdress of a pharaoh. It was regarded as a spiritual guardian. I wondered if this was, in its own way, the talisman for the gold-bearing reef. Naturally, we were keen to find out if there was any cultural or spiritual significance, even a dreaming story, with The Monument.

Despite several enquiries with some locals, particularly Aboriginal elders, we were only able to find some basic information. Not surprisingly, it seems that The Monument stands on a sacred or mythological site, forming part of Yulluna country, and is potentially the boundary between women's and men's country. Given the shape of the top part of the rock formation, which can also appear to look like a phallus, Mount Isa local Joe Rogers (although not from the

Pharaoh's head, formally known as The Monument, on a triangulated mound, near Dajarra, Queensland, is another piece of the puzzle that comes to life from Lasseter's Diary. Considerable erosion has taken place since bushman Joseph Harding travelled through there over a century ago.

Yulluna people his grandfather, First World War digger Peter Craigie, raised his family at Dajarra) indicated that it relates to 'man's business' and would be an area where initiations would take place.

Although there are some similar-looking rock formations around the area, which are continually being carved by erosion, some believe that The Monument was shaped by ancient ancestors. However, if perceiving it to look like a galah, perhaps the spiritual significance relates to showing something off and/or silly antics. That has certainly been my experience with Lasseter's Reef.

As of March 2020, the EPM had been granted for the 225 square kilometres surrounding a section of the reef on the border of Queensland and the Northern Territory. Prior to that, the application was advertised, especially since the Aboriginal people in that area have a right to negotiate. As per the EPM, they have agreed to us having that right under Native Title Protection Conditions, and the land owner, whom we get along well with, is aware of our intentions.

Although the area in the Diamantina region takes in far more than what is actually required, as Doug Wilson and I have learned from previous experience, it is better to have it covered from the outset. The thing about getting involved with minerals and exploration is that significant capital is required. However, when it has come to doing anything more with Lasseter's Reef in the past, it has been people's unscrupulous and avaricious motives that time and again would put a stop to it. It was as if the land or the universe was preventing us from getting to the needle until the right combination of people — people with integrity — were in place. Now that there are three of us who have come together, it seems to be the best mix with Jason, who, despite me doubting his genuine interest at the beginning, has been invaluable with his unwavering enthusiasm, support and belief.

Ever since I first watched *The Legend of Lasseter* documentary in 1980, little did I know that it would be a forty-year journey with Lasseter's Reef. As frustrating as it has been at times, it seems to be the way things had to be done, especially with the land showing me where the reef was in a certain way and at a certain time. If I ever tried to force things, it wouldn't happen. But if I simply became curious about something, or let things go, another piece of the puzzle would fall into place. It was another step closer to revealing the truth — the whole story — which I believe has been my purpose.

There's no doubt that sticking to the simple facts is what helped me. In essence, everything has always revolved around those three hills 'that could not be mistaken', because once I found those, everything else had to come together, but only if I was in the right area. Just like a crime scene, if you're in the right place, you will find evidence, but if you're not, you won't find anything.

Although the needle is still yet to be found, no matter how much gold there might be out there, if you don't have the landmarks, you don't have Lasseter's Reef. With that in mind, I've realised that there are actually two distinct parts to the reef. Firstly, there's the approximately 16 kilometre-long quartz-bearing reef itself — Lasseter's Reef (the haystack). Secondly, there's possibly what Lasseter (courtesy of Harding) described as the 3 ounces of gold per ton embedded somewhere within a section of it — Lasseter's gold (the needle). So whenever people now ask me about the legendary reef, I ask them, 'Do you want to find Lasseter's Reef, or Lasseter's gold?' While some regard the reef and gold as one in the same, there is a marked difference.

Based on all of my research and first-hand experience over the years, I have found Lasseter's Reef. Whether the reef is or isn't an El Dorado, is yet to be determined, but even if it has 4 grams of gold per ton, it is worth pursuing. Strange as it may seem, like vivid pictures in my mind, I know where the needle is, but given the enormity of the reef and the way events have unfolded, so far it has been difficult to get there.

We already know that a section of the reef to the north is on sacred land, while another section, where the needle may very well be, could be in the Ethabuka Reserve. Nestled in the Simpson Desert, the former cattle station, which is now a vast 215,500 hectare conservation reserve, borders the eastern, northern and southern area of where we have acquired the permit. And the Munga-Thirri National Park is within close proximity. Maybe the sacred guardian wants the needle to remain as is — intact and sacrosanct. If that is how it is meant to be, I respect that.

Aside from the section of the reef that we have obtained the EPM for being gold and silver positive, based on the most recent samples that have been taken from it, there are indications of copper and highly sought after lithium. It is possible that part of the reef could be rich in other ways. Currently, the search is on for a suitable mining company.

Then, of course, there's the gazillion-dollar question: what will be done with the profits generated from Lasseter's Reef? Besides paying off the mortgage, should the reef be extremely lucrative, the intention is that the gold, or even lithium, will make a meaningful difference. It will be put back to where it is needed most.

Apart from the reef being of social and economic benefit to local communities such as Boulia, Dajarra and Glenormiston, I would like to see some of the money be invested closer to home, including the proposed Melton Hospital. Although the hospital is currently in the discussion and planning stage, like the additional ambulance services that I advocated for, accessible, quality and adequate medical services are sorely needed. Therefore, it could be a wing, an operating theatre or specialist department that some of the money goes towards.

And given my family's near brush with homelessness, it would be terrific to establish emergency accommodation and provide basic educational services to help those in need get back on track and become self-sufficient. I've always believed that it is important to give everyone, no matter what they have been through, a sense of support and connection. Doesn't everyone have the right to live comfortably, or at least have the opportunity to improve their quality of life? Being in a dire or what may seem to be a hopeless situation can happen to anyone one of us, and instantaneously. I will always be grateful to those who helped me when I needed it, and now I would like to pay it forward.

With that in mind, and given I didn't complete my secondary schooling (I left at the end of Form 3), I would love to establish a scholarship at my former high school, Eltham

High School. I would like to provide others, especially those who may be facing hardship, with the opportunity to complete their education. If I had one regret in life, it was that I didn't finish mine.

But it is these three key things that I have always wanted to create and contribute to, and Lasseter's Reef could help achieve them. To me, there's no point having money for the sake of it. I've always believed that when you share money around, it can do a lot of good.

To this day, a lot of people look at me strangely when I say that it isn't about the gold, or I don't care if I don't get anything out of it. They think that isn't normal, but it isn't their normal. For me, anything beyond proving that the reef exists is an absolute bonus. It means I can do a lot more that I would like to do, and it's not just for me but for many others.

Even when Jason and I had our initial discussions about collaborating with Lasseter's Reef, he was keen to donate a certain amount of money to a charity. That or he suggested we start our own foundation, something that we could all do together to give back to society at large. That's when I knew we were on the same track.

Jason, who attributes his mum as being the one to instil the value of giving in him, was a single father at one stage and is particularly passionate about seeing single fathers gain equal access to their children and being compassionately supported through what is both a distressing and prohibitively costly process. Given the nature of his pawn shop business, he sees far too many people, day in and day out, struggling to keep their families together. He believes that what is currently provided for single fathers is insufficient, therefore envisions a support service that will help to overcome this. Like me, Jason believes that everyone is entitled to receiving help equally and fairly.

In addition, Doug and I would love to see a monument placed in Boulia with an inscription that briefly retells the legend of Lasseter's Reef and how the true story originates from the region. Despite Doug withdrawing his involvement from the mineral exploration side of Lasseter's Reef (he will assist as needed), perhaps his wishes will be granted.

Depending how things evolve, the reef isn't necessarily going to be strictly off limits to the public. At the same time, it needs to be done in consultation with the community and landowners, who are already embracing what we intend to do. Perhaps scenic flights from Boulia can take place over Lasseter's Reef and the surrounding landscape. It would also be terrific to establish an immersive museum. They would be a boon for tourism.

At the time of going to print, Plutonic Limited, a Melbourne-based mineral resources company, has approached us about acquiring the EPM for Lasseter's Reef. We look forward to seeing what unfolds.

In many ways, the reef itself has become like an intersection — a meeting point, whereby it is the final chapter for the wide-ranging narratives that have amassed for the last ninety years. Add to that how Australia is the outback, yet is slowly changing to the point that we are losing it. With Lasseter's Reef being in the expansive desolateness, my hope is that it will help to put the real Australia back into perspective: it is, after all, something to be cherished.

My sentiments about the reef contrast those of Dick Smith, who, in an article that was published in the 150th edition of *Australian Geographic* in 2019, said that he remained 'sceptical' about its existence. Yet he also hoped that the search for Australia's 'Holy Grail' would 'continue forever':

> I want people to keep searching for it because it is the most wonderful Australian romantic mystery. It's our El Dorado ... And it's very important for our country to have people like Harold Lasseter, who, for me, was an extraordinary adventurer who genuinely believed there was a reef out there and went out there to search for it ... I quite like the idea of

it being out there but never able to be found because you can keep searching for it.

Amid his somewhat contradictory statement, and encouraging people to go on an unnecessary wild goose chase, ironically Smith still believes 'the reef could be found one day'.[2]

Since the mystery of Lasseter's reef has been solved, Doug, Jason and I feel that it is fitting for the reef to remain named as is. Although the story was always Harding's to begin with, it was Lasseter, who, in his own peculiar way, brought the fabulous gold reef to the nation's attention, then died for his efforts.

Then again, maybe the land will offer its wisdom or a new insight, because when you listen closely enough, that's what it does. It is the lore of the land.

ENDNOTES

INTRODUCTION

1 Coote (1934), 86.
2 Roosevelt (1910).

CHAPTER 1: THE CURIOUS CASE OF LASSETER

1 Coote (1934), 25-27.
2 Ibid.
3 NAA B2455 (1916).
4 Lasseter (1929), NAA: A1, 1930/512.
5 Lasseter (1930), NAA: A786, C64/7.

CHAPTER 2: A BEACON OF HOPE

1 Coote (1934), 25-27.
2 Bailey (1947), 1.
3 Coote (1934), 36.
4 Bailey, E. (1979).
5 Lasseter (1930), NAA: A786, C64/7.
6 Blakeley (1984), 99-101.
7 Taylor (1979).
8 Coote (1934).

CHAPTER 3: TRAGEDY STRIKES

1 Johns' statement to Ernestine Hill (1932).
2 Lasseter (1930ca. 1931).
3 Ibid.
4 Ibid.
5 Bailey (1947), as per the unpublished manuscript *History of Lasseter's Reef*.
6 Lloyd (1948), 2.

CHAPTER 4: THE SEARCH BEGINS

1 Idriess (1931), 435.
2 Coote (1934), 86.
3 Bernoth (1992).

CHAPTER 5: REEF REALITY

1 State Library South Australia.

CHAPTER 6: DIGGING DEEPER

1 VIC Death Cert. no. 10036/1899.
2 Hubbard (1993), 30.
3 *Colac Herald* (1896), as cited in Hubbard (1993), 74-77.
4 Hubbard (1993), 88-89.
5 Ibid., 187.
6 Ibid., 186.
7 NAA B2455.
8 Hubbard (1993), 26.
9 Bureau of Immigration and Naturalization, USA (1907).
10 Caledonian Maritime Research Trust.
11 Hubbard (1993), 22.
12 NAA A6180, 19/6/74/41.
13 Hubbard (1993), 32.
14 Ibid., 190.
15 Coote (1934), 29.
16 Hubbard (1993), 171.
17 Lasseter (1914).
18 NAA B2455 (1916).
19 Ibid.
20 Hubbard (1993), 56.
21 Ibid., 62.
22 Ibid., 58.
23 NAA B2455 (1916).
24 Ibid.
25 Ibid.
26 Sands & McDougall's South Australian Directory (1917).
27 NAA B2455 (1916).
28 Hubbard (1993), 35.
29 Ibid., 125.
30 Ibid., 110.
31 Ibid., 187.

32 Ibid., 107-108.

CHAPTER 7: CONSISTENT DISCREPANCIES

1 Hubbard (1993), 202.
2 Marshall-Stoneking (1989), 199.
3 Hubbard (1993), 98.
4 *Australian, Coal, Shipping, Steel and the Harbour* (1929), as cited in Hubbard (1993), 34.
5 Lasseteria.
6 Hubbard (1993), 155-158.
7 England (2003), 38.
8 Coote (1934), 41-47.
9 Blakeley (1984), 9.
10 Ibid.
11 Coote (1934), 70 & 71.
12 Blakeley (1984), 100.
13 Ibid.
14 Ibid., 20.
15 Ibid., 27.
16 Ibid., 86.

CHAPTER 8: WHO WAS HARDING?

1 Blakeley (1984), 181.
2 Ibid.
3 AAS (1899), A1/1 Item 12/10343.
4 *Mail* (1924), 1.
5 *Register* (1925), 11.
6 Ibid.
7 *Mail* (1924), 1.
8 *Register* (1925), 11.
9 Ibid.
10 Ibid.
11 Kimber (1986), 8.
12 Ibid.
13 SAA 790/1892/401.
14 Kimber (1986), 8.
15 Newland (1877), 6-7, as cited in Kimber (1986), 8.
16 Kimber (1986), 8.
17 Ibid.
18 Ibid., 9.

19 Coulthard (1903), 47 &71, as transcribed by Kate Holmes (1988).
20 Kimber (1986), 9.
21 Ibid., 79-80.
22 Ibid., 26.
23 *Mail* (1924), 1.

CHAPTER 9: A DEGREE OF SEPARATION

1 Kimber (1986), 86-87.
2 Ibid., 87-88.
3 *Chronicle* (1928), 22.
4 *Register* (1925), 11.
5 *Mail* (1924).

CHAPTER 10: RETURNING TO THE REEF

1 Lasseter (1930ca. 1931).

CHAPTER 11: DOWN TO A BEARING

1 Queensland Police Service (2019).
2 Smith (2003), 19-20.

CHAPTER 13: UNEXPECTED REUNION

1 Lockwood (1999).
2 *Australian* (2011).

CHAPTER 16: IN THREES

1 Lasseter (1930ca. 1931).
2 Clacherty (1989), 32.
3 Marshall-Stoneking (1989).
4 NAA: D1915, SA1268.
5 Clark (2015), 177.
6 Ibid.
7 Clark (2019), 220.
8 Ibid., 238.
9 Ibid., 239.

CHAPTER 17: AS GOOD AS GOLD

1 Lasseter (1930ca. 1931).
2 The Yowie Man (2019).

SOURCES

Allen, Barry. "This is Lasseter's Reef", *People* magazine, Sydney, 31 Aug. 1994.

Australian Archives Series A1/1 Item 12/10343

Australian Coal, Shipping, Steel and the Harbour, Sydney, 2 Sept. 1929.

Bailey, John, *Bailey Papers*, Mitchell Library, State Library of New South Wales, Sydney, 1945–1947.

Bailey, John, "History of Lasseter's Reef, and an explanation of the two expeditions despatched to Central Australia", unpublished manuscript dated 26 Sept., 1947, State Library of New South Wales, Sydney, A2753.

Bernoth, Ardyn. "Lasseter Quest May Be Solved", *Sunday Herald Sun*, Melbourne, 5 Jan. 1992.

Blakeley, Fred, and edited by Frances Wheelhouse and Mary Mansfield. *Lasseter's Dream of Millions*: *New Light on the Lost Gold Reef*, (2nd edition), Transpareon Press, Sydney, 1984.

Brown, Warren. *Lasseter's Gold*, Hachette Australia, Sydney, 2015.

Bureau of Immigration & Naturalization, USA, 1907.

C.A.G.E Papers, National Archives of Australia, Canberra.

Caledonian Maritime Research Trust. An online database for Scottish built ships. https://www.clydeships.co.uk/

Cartwright, Max. *Ayers Rock to the Petermanns: Legend of Lasseter*, Alice Springs, 1991.

Clacherty, Desmond R. *On Lasseter's Trail*, Malvern Press, Malvern, 1989.

Clark, Chris. *Olof's Suitcase: Lasseter's Reef Mystery Solved*, Echo Books, Geelong, 2015.

Clark, Chris. *The Truth About Lasseter: Why His Elusive Gold Reef Never Existed*, Echo Books, Geelong, 2019.

Coote, Errol. *Hell's Airport and Lasseter's Lost Legacy*, Peterman Press, Sydney, 1934.

Coulthard, William and Kate Holmes. *Diary of William Coulthard 1903.* Transcribed and annotated by Kate Holmes April/June 1988. https://territorystories.nt.gov.au/10070/449299/0/0

England, Kathryn. *Lasseter: the Man, the legend, the gold.* Omnibus Books, Norwood, 2003.

"From the Vault — Rewan: A Stud Farm for Breeding Police Horses", Queensland Police Service, July 2019. https://mypolice.qld.gov.au/museum/2019/07/02/from-the-vault-rewan-a-stud-farm-for-breeding-police-horses/

Gates, Josh. *Expedition Unknown*, "Lasseter's Gold", Ping Pong Productions for the Travel Channel, Glendale, 2017.

"Gold Seekers for Central Australia", *Sunday Times* (Perth), 16 Aug. 1931, 1, in Trove [online database], accessed 15 December 2019. https://trove.nla.gov.au/newspaper/page/4375080

Hill, Ernestine. *About Lasseter: Paul John's Statement*, Elizabeth, 1932 (as printed by Scrivener Press, 1968).

Holmes, Kate and University of Sydney. "The White Range settlement area, Arltunga Goldfield, Northern Territory: A look at the life style of an isolated mining area using written and archaeological records" thesis, Sydney, 1980.

Hubbard, Murray. *The Search for Harold Lasseter: The True Story of the Man Behind the Myths*, Angus & Robertson, Sydney, 1993.

Idriess, Ion L. *Lasseter's Last Ride in Ion Idriess's Greatest Stories*, Angus & Robertson, Sydney, 1931 (1986 edition).

Kimber, Richard. *Man from Arltunga*, Hesperian Press, Carlisle, 1986.

King, Jack. *Bush Tucker Man: Stories of Survival*, "Gold Fever", ABC Television, Sydney 1996.

Lasseter, Harold Bell. *Lasseter's Diary*, facsimile edition by Angus & Robertson, Sydney, 1986. (Original Harold Lasseter diary with fragments held by State Library of NSW, MLMSS 3269 (Safe 2/10), 1930 – ca. 1931.)

"Last of the Old-Timers", the *Mail* (Adelaide), 12 Apr. 1924, 1, in Trove [online database], accessed 11 Mar. 2019. http://nla.gov.au/nla.news-article63861905

Lockwood, Kim. "Desert of Dreams", *Herald Sun Weekend*, Melbourne, 19 Jun. 1999.

Marsden, Susan. *South Australian State Historic Preservation Plan: Historical Guidelines*, South Australian Department of Environment and Planning, 1980 (1984 edition).

Marshall, Lloyd, "The Riddle of Lasseter's Reef", *Daily News* (Perth), 9 Aug. 1948, 2, in Trove [online database], accessed 9 Feb. 2019.

Marshall-Stoneking, Billy. *Lasseter in Quest of Gold*, Hodder & Stroughton, Sydney. 1985 (1994 edition).

"M.J. Harding", the *Chronicle* (Adelaide), 14 Jan. 1928, 22, in Trove [online database], accessed 11 Mar. 2019. http://nla.gov.au/nla.news-page8664170

"Mr Joseph Harding Reminiscent", the *Register* (Adelaide), 29 Aug. 1925, 11, in Trove [online database], accessed 11 Mar. 2019. http://nla.gov.au/nla.news-article165709812

National Archives of Australia (NAA)

NAA: A1, 1930/512 — LHB Lasseter: auriferous areas of Central Australia

NAA: A786, C64/7 — Gold Mining, Central Australia

NAA: A6180, 19/6/74/41 — Relic: certificate stating Lasseter passed surveying course

NAA: B2455, Lasseter Lewis Hubert, service number 23636 https://recordsearch.naa.gov.au/SearchNRetrieve/Interface/ViewImage.aspx?B=8334260

NAA: D1915, SA1268, Johanson Olaf Emanuel http://www.naa.gov.au/go.aspx?i=882353

Newland, Simpson. *The Far North Country*, Burden & Bonython, Adelaide, 1887.

Phelps Citizen, New York, 19 May 1914.

Registrar of Births, Deaths and Marriages Adelaide (Barossa District): Death Certificate 496, 12 Jan. 1928.

Robinson, Lee. *The Legend of Lasseter*, John McCallum Productions for the Seven Network, Sydney, 1979.

Roosevelt, Theodore. "The Man in the Arena" speech, Paris, 1910.

Ross, Robert. Lasseteria.com. An online encyclopaedia for Lasseter's Reef, 1999-2006.

Sands & McDougall's South Australian Directory, 1917.

South Australian Archives (SAA)

SAA GRG 67/14, 1890.

SAA 790 — 1892/401.

Smith, Libby. *Carnarvon Station: A History of European Settlement since 1863*. Bush Heritage Australia. 2003. https://www.bushheritage.org.au/getmedia/82f62f14-f8c6-402e-8cfd-35c304b35561/Carnarvon-history-Libby-Smith

Stapleton, Austin. *Lasseter Did Not Lie!*, Investigator Press, Hawthorndene, 1981.

State Library of South Australia, Adelaide https://www.samemory.sa.gov.au/site/page.cfm?u=505

Testa, Angie, and Bill Decarli. *A Dead Man's Dream: Lasseter's Reef Found*, Hesperian Press, Carlisle, 2005.

Walker, Luke. *Lasseter's Bones*, Scribble Films, Melbourne, 2012.

Yowie Man, Tim (the). "Lasseter's Reef. Will It Ever Be Found?" *Australian Geographic*, Sydney, May-June 2019.

Acknowledgements

Uncovering the mystery surrounding Lasseter's Reef has been filled with stops and starts, twists and turns. In the end, it has been the invaluable contributions, whether large or small, from the various people that I have encountered along the way that have helped me take a step closer to the truth. Every one of them is just as much a part of its story, and for that I thank them from the bottom of my heart.

Many thanks to Jason Faddoul for his wholehearted belief and significant investment in this story. His assistance and tenacity are the reason for reigniting my passion — confirming that Lasseter's Reef does in fact exist.

A special mention goes to Doug Wilson for being a loyal friend and believing in me right from the start, all those years ago. His expert geological knowledge, understanding and generosity of time are a huge part of all of this coming together.

I am immensely grateful for Kristin Lee helping me tell my story and for asking the right questions at the right time. Her inquisitiveness, open-mindedness and intuition are what helped me put the last pieces of this long, convoluted puzzle together.

To my daughter Alycia for helping find the right Joseph Harding by hunting through the various family trees of those men with the same name. For without him, or her tireless efforts, the true origins of Lasseter's Reef would have remained a mystery.

To my son Daniel for being a rock and for helping me to express what I felt, especially when I struggled to find the words when I needed them. I am also grateful for him transcribing the audio recordings from my 1991 trip to Lasseter's Reef.

And to my beautiful wife Pat for her faith, courage and patience, and unconditional love and support. Without her, my journey would never have even begun, and my dream of proving that Lasseter's Reef exists would never have come true. For this I can never thank her enough.

Many thanks to my nephew Michael Valle for joining me on the maiden voyage in the Land Rover to the Australian outback, and for making that backbreaking Hay River crossing possible. Together we found the three hills that could 'not be mistaken'. Most of all, he was part of the pebble that rolled into the avalanche of solving this great Australian mystery.

To my good friend Lee Shawsmith for being there when times were tough on the second trip to Lasseter's Reef, especially since they seemed like unfavorable odds. Thanks also to all of the members of the original 1993 syndicate whose support and enthusiasm allowed me to achieve so much after that trip. Their efforts started a chain of events that led the story to where it is today.

To the staff members at the State Records of South Australia, the National Archives of Australia in Canberra, the Northern Territory Archives Service, the State Library of New South Wales and what was previously known as the Department of Mines in Canberra for their assistance, patience and knowledge with helping me locate vital information when needed. Each piece, over time, simply led us in the right direction.

To the staff at the Births, Deaths and Marriages Registration Office of Adelaide for finding the death certificate for the correct Joseph Harding. And thanks to Stephen Kime at the Seven Network for sourcing the 1979 *Legend of Lasseter* documentary from the archives. To Duncan Leask at the Queensland Police Museum for locating historical maps of Carnarvon, Queensland, and for sharing insights about Rewan.

To Australian military historian Chris Clark for permission to reproduce an image of his grandfather Olof Johanson and for pointing out documentation pertaining to Olof's place of residence while in Adelaide. Thanks also to Jan Hall from the National Archives of Australia for confirming the details of this documentation.

Many thanks go to Bob Lasseter for taking the time to respond to my occasional correspondence over the years and for permission to reproduce an image of the telegram Olof Johanson sent to Bob's father, Harold Lasseter, in June 1930. Bob and I may not have agreed on where Lasseter's Reef was located or how it was discovered in the first place, but we both shared a sincere belief that his father was aware of its existence.

To the State Library of South Australia and Margot Way at the Royal Adelaide Hospital Heritage Office for helping to clarify details about the location and formal and informal names of Adelaide's public hospital. That in itself was starting to become its own mystery. To John Claxton at the Army Museum of South Australia, Keswick Barracks, for shedding light on the 7th Australian General Hospital and the 17th Australian Auxiliary Hospital.

To Scott Blacket from the Boulia Caravan Park for his unwavering enthusiasm and for connecting us with various people, both near and far, especially those who had insights about past events with the quartz-bearing reef. And a special thank you to Phillip Anderson for sharing his father's lesser-known story about the Aboriginal people at Tobermorey Station and their discovery of gold specimens near the reef.

Thanks to pilot Doug Pratt for ensuring I got to live to tell the baffling tale, in spite of the mishaps on the 2018 trip. Thanks also to cattle farmer and Boulia Shire councillor Sam Beauchamp for coming to our aid when the plane ran out of fuel, and for embracing all the good that Lasseter's Reef can bring to the community. With that in mind, thank you to the people of Boulia who understand its cultural and economic significance.

To Joe Rogers and Shorty Rogers for providing some basic insight about The Monument, near Dajarra in Queensland.

I would like to thank Hesperian Press for permission to quote from the *Man from Arltunga* and for allowing me to re-tell parts of my story in another way. Many thanks to Des Clacherty and his daughter Sarah for permission to quote from *On Lasseter's Trail* and to *Australian Geographic's* Editor-in-chief, Chrissie Goldrick, for permission to quote from an article that appeared in the 150th edition of the publication.

To artist Belinda Williams, I am most grateful for her amazing artistic contributions to this book and, on a more personal note, for helping me with my own trials and tribulations. And thanks to Kerwin Ross for digitising the artwork.

I am also eternally grateful to Malcom Brown, Karen Cottrell, Jenny and Tim Cottrell, Kevin Moloney, Sophie Wajsman and Leonie Wilkie for providing invaluable feedback for the initial draft of this comprehensive story.

To Dan Kelly and the team at Boolarong Press, I would like to express my sincere appreciation for their incredible efforts with helping get this book out into the world. Thank you for believing in the story and for giving it the chance to be shared in its entirety.

And a special thank you to Lasseter's Reef for teaching me so much about the land and myself — and for putting the past, present and future into clearer perspective.

About the Authors

Bill Decarli is an Australian explorer and Vietnam veteran who has spent the best part of forty years proving that the elusive Lasseter's Reef *does* exist. A man of integrity and honour, he believes in acknowledging people's contributions and that we are all here for a purpose: to leave our own legacy, understand the gift of generosity and to learn from and share the wisdom of our life experiences. Bill has been interviewed in the *Herald Sun*, was included in the book *Fabulous Furphies: 10 Great Myths from Australia's Past*, and in 2017 appeared on American adventure series *Expedition Unknown*. He is the co-author of *A Dead Man's Dream: Lasseter's Reef Found* (Hesperian Press, 2005). When the time comes for this persistent adventurer and modern-day storyteller, he would like his headstone to read: 'There, I told you so'. The father of four and grandfather of three lives in Melbourne, Australia.

Kristin Lee is a writer and former TV producer who has a penchant for documenting creative disruptors and exploring the connection between the environments in which we live and how they shape who we are. Her stories have appeared in leading Australian print and online publications including *The Age*, Qantas inflight magazine and *The Australian*. She has also worked with primetime Australian TV productions and documentaries including *The Great Outdoors*, *What's Good For You* and *Secret Millionaire*. A country girl at heart, Kristin lives in the Dandenong Ranges of Victoria, Australia.